Moments In Time

STORIES ABOUT ARTISTS AND SONGS OF THE 50S, 60S, AND 70S.

FOR FANS OF MUSIC ... FROM A MUSIC FAN

TOM LOCKE

TSPA THE SELF PUBLISHING AGENCY, INC.

Tom Locke

Moments In Time

TSPA The Self Publishing Agency, Inc.

Copyright © 2021 by Tom Locke

First Edition

Softcover ISBN: 978-1-7778273-0-4
Electronic ISBN: 978-1-7778273-1-1

Cover & Book Design | Kristy Twellmann Hill

Editor | Trevor McMonagle

Publishing Support | TSPA The Self Publishing Agency, Inc.

DEDICATION

To music fans everywhere who embraced and still embrace the sounds of the 50s, 60s, and 70s.

TABLE OF CONTENTS

STREET CORNER HARMONY

GROUP DYNAMICS

THE GIRLS WITH THE BIGGEST HITS

FOREWORD

I had the good fortune to be introduced to Tom Locke in the early 80s by my lifelong friend, Frank Van de Ven, whom I've known since we both worked at CFCF Radio in Montreal in the early 70s, and again in 1975 at CJFM-FM in Montreal. As fate would have it, Tom and Frank were business colleagues.

When I met Tom, I was Vice-President Artist & Repertoire with A&M Records Canada and had already experienced some defining moments in my career through the signing of a number of talented artists, including the prolific singer/songwriter, Bryan Adams.

That first meeting with Tom evolved into both a personal friendship and professional relationship that spans well over thirty years so far. Tom's background in the entertainment field and his passion for music complements my radio and music industry experience and my own passion for great music and the artists who create it.

Back in the mid-80s, Tom created and recorded a few demos of a great concept he had for a short entertainment audio feature, which came to be known as "Moments In Time." Tom shared this with me in the late 90s while I was in the midst of developing and launching an oldies radio show, *Treasure Island Oldies*. The show debuted online on May 3, 1997, and in May 2021, celebrated its 24th anniversary.

In 2000, Tom and I decided to join forces and add "Moments In Time" as a weekly feature to my show. Week after week, listeners let me know how much they enjoy these feature segments, which delve into the background of an artist's hit song, and then conclude with the playing of the song itself.

When you read this book of scripts, you'll note Tom's meticulous research, and his very entertaining style of writing that makes this book readable and enjoyable from cover to cover, in either direction.

So again, 1 say, "Thank you, Frank" for introducing me to Tom.

Enjoy!

Michael Godin
Treasure Island Oldies
The Home of Lost Treasures
Spring 2021

Tom & Michael circa 2003

PREFACE

This book is the culmination of a journey that started back in 1986 with an idea I had about creating a legacy to the music that shaped my life, and a desire to share this legacy in an entertaining and informative way with others.

But first, the pre-journey. Growing up in the 50s and 60s in Toronto, we had radio as a staple at our house. Living in a "border" town we were privy to many major U.S. radio and TV stations and their programs. It was one of those U.S. radio programs that gave me the inspiration for my legacy  idea. That program was called *The Rest of the Story,* hosted by the incomparable newscaster Paul Harvey, who originated this nationally sponsored segment out of Chicago. His tag line "And now you know the rest of the story" stayed in my mind.

Embracing this format, I designed a five-minute teaser segment about music to be heard on the radio during drive times to and from work. An interesting musical fact or period of time would be introduced for the listener to ponder during a commercial break. After the commercial break, the listener would get "the rest of the story," culminating in the playing of the record mysteriously featured in the segment.

In April 1986, Vancouver radio deejay Bert Gordon voiced over a demo of five segments I had written. To test the waters, I entrusted one of my clients, the producer of K-tel's oldies music compilations, to give the demo a listen. His response: "I wish there were more. I really enjoyed them."

As luck would have it, in that same year, my company was invited to join the International Quorum of Motion Picture Producers and I soon ended up befriending its Nashville member, Curt Hahn, CEO of Film House. Hahn's company does the majority of TV commercials to promote radio stations all around the world. He graciously bounced my concept and demo off his experienced crew as well as a select number of his clients.

What I got back was deflating. Radio stations wanted syndicated music shows of a minimum of one hour – preferably three or four hours. Those were the days of Dick Bartley's *Rock and Roll's Greatest Hits* and Casey Kasem's *American Top 40*. Nobody wanted "sound bites" as my five-minute segments were described back then.

I put my idea on the shelf for eight years. Then *Treasure Island Oldies* came along, the brainchild of my good and trusted friend, Michael Godin, who immediately saw this as a perfect feature segment for his weekly Internet music radio show.

In August 2000, complete with Sorrells Pickard Gourmet Peanut Butter as a sponsor, we launched my five-minute feature in the third hour of Michael's show. It was well-received by his listening audience; ironically, people were now into "sound bites."

These weekly "Moments In Time," best described as curated walks down memory lane, have been playing weekly on *Treasure Island Oldies* and its worldwide affiliate stations for over twenty years.

The impetus for the book was to honor this milestone by sharing a selection of segments that have aired on *Treasure Island Oldies* over these years.

Tom Locke
Spring 2021

HOW TO READ & ENJOY THIS BOOK

When reading this book, **have some fun**, and imagine that it is you behind the microphone unveiling these stories of artists and songs of the **50s, 60s, and 70s**.

These stories have been modified from their radio script versions with the symbol ✴✴✴✴✴ representing a **commercial break**.

At the end of each two-page story, the featured song is bolded. To listen to this song, simply **place your smartphone camera (like you're going to take a photo) over the QR code**. This will link you directly to it.

References to dates in the stories should be taken in context with the date the story first aired on *Treasure Island Oldies*. The airdate follows the title of each "Moments In Time" segment.

When it comes to the names of artists and the title of songs, they are consistent with those listed in Joel Whitburn's ***Top Pop Singles 1955 to 1999***.

THE EARLY DAYS OF
ROCK & ROLL

Rock & Roll originated in the United States during the late 1940s and early 1950s from musical styles such as gospel, jump blues, jazz, boogie woogie, rhythm & blues (R&B), and country. It was a turn-on to the youth of the day, a new demographic referred to as the "Teenager," a group who had access to radios and money to buy the records they wanted to hear.

The music was colorless to them and the demand for "their" music went nationwide in no time.

The following ten segments in this chapter cover the impact of the late 40s and early 50s, the influences of many of the established genres, and some of Rock & Roll's lesser-known pioneers.

THE POWER OF AN HOUR
Aired in June 2001

When a song from the early days of Rock & Roll is referred to as being a "classic," you can rest assured that it has the following three attributes: it sounds as fresh and cool as the day it charted, it has meaningful lyrics, and its vocals are in sync with the music.

Fifty years ago in 1951, a black group released such a classic. It was an R&B tune that, in addition to being a national hit that year, became and has remained one of the unofficial go-to songs of the state dance of South Carolina.

*****

In 1950, a black gospel ensemble appeared on the *Arthur Godfrey and His Friends* TV show. After a while, due to the unique voice of its lead singer, Clyde McPhatter, the group started singing more blues numbers. This led them to a contract with Federal Records. One year later they had a national hit on their hands – a record that, many years later, became a contender for the title of being the first Rock & Roll record ever made.

Ironically, the lead on this recording, which has truly passed the test of time, was the group's bass singer, Bill Brown, not Clyde McPhatter. The song's lyrics were somewhat suggestive, and many radio stations banned it at the time. However, it had a great beat and, in the Carolinas, the kids loved to dance the Shag to it.

The Shag became the official state dance of South Carolina in 1984. In the 90s there was a move afoot to make it the state dance of North Carolina as well. The Shag has been described as a partner dance that is an offshoot of the Carolina Jitterbug and its predecessor, the Little Apple (the white version of the Big Apple that surfaced in Columbia, South Carolina around 1937).

In the 80s, a revival of the dance took hold in the South. Every year in April and September, thousands of "shaggers" of all ages, shapes and sizes head for the "Beach" in South Carolina for a week of dancing and partying at S.O.S.

S.O.S. stands for the Society Of Stranders, in recognition of the Grand Strand, the famous beaches on the coast of the Carolinas.

So the next time you're in North Myrtle Beach, stop in at Fat Harold's and either put a quarter in the jukebox or ask the deejay to play this great 50-year-old shaggin' tune by Billy Ward And His Dominoes – **"Sixty Minute Man."**

 SIXTY MINUTE MAN

Open your smartphone camera & scan this QR code to listen to the song.

AIN'T IT THE TRUTH
Aired in March 2008

In February we paid tribute to Ritchie Valens, Buddy Holly and the Big Bopper. The Big Bopper, of course, was known for his chartbusting novelty hit, "Chantilly Lace," which debuted in August of 1958 and remained on the charts for 25 weeks.

His untimely death in that horrible plane crash on February 3, 1959 cut short a promising career as a performer and a songwriter. Some claim that he would have had more hits if he had been alive to promote additional recordings after "Chantilly Lace" had peaked on the charts.

We are going to let you be the judge of that when you listen to another recording from his album (also titled *Chantilly Lace*).

*****

The Big Bopper was born Jiles Perry Richardson in 1930 in Sabina Pass, Texas. Known to his friends as J.P. or Jape, he eventually became a disc jockey in Beaumont, Texas.

In the late 50s, he became interested in songwriting and performing, coining his own name, the Big Bopper, after the latest dance craze, the Bop.

In May 1957, the Big Bopper played 1,821 records back-to-back on the radio during a marathon show lasting five days, two hours and eight minutes – he beat the old record for continuous broadcasting by eight minutes.

Away from the radio, he played guitar and wrote songs, one of which was "Running Bear" that Johnny Preston took to #1 in 1960.

The Big Bopper became a serious performer after being discovered by Harold "Pappy" Daily. Soon after, "Chantilly Lace" hit the airwaves and his album began to sell.

His untimely death at the age of 28 was tragic. If he had been around to promote more of his records off that album, he would have undoubtedly had more hits.

A case in point is this lost treasure being heard for the first time on *Treasure Island Oldies*. If he were alive today, the Big Bopper would support our claim about his talent by proclaiming "**It's The Truth Ruth**."

IT'S THE
TRUTH RUTH

Open your smartphone camera & scan this QR code to listen to the song.

THE DRESS CODE OF THE 50S

Aired in February 2006

In 1979 recording artist Robert John resurfaced on the Billboard charts with a smooth, self-composed pop ballad, "Sad Eyes," which went all the way to #1.

According to author Fred Bronson who writes in his *Billboard Book Of Number One Hits*: "Robert John waited longer than any other artist for a number one record. From the time of his first appearance on the Hot 100 on November 10, 1958, to the time he topped the chart on October 6, 1979, was 20 years and 11 months. That record was eventually broken by Tina Turner (with 'What's Love Got To Do With It')."

So what was Robert John's first entry on the Billboard charts in 1958?

*****

Robert John was born in Brooklyn, New York in 1946. After kicking around the fringe of the music industry for 14 years, he surprised many in the industry in 1971 with a #3 smash hit, a remake of "The Lion Sleeps Tonight," produced by Hank Medress, who had sung on the Tokens' version of that same song which went to #1 in 1961.

This record confirmed that his vocal range hadn't changed much since his first appearance on the charts in 1958.

In addition to his staying power, perhaps dropping his surname and going simply with his first two names, Robert John, had something to do with his ultimate success.

You see when Robert John first hit the charts in 1958 at the age of 12, he was known as Bobby Pedrick, Jr. Because of his #1 hit with "Sad Eyes" in 1979, his breakout record has become a much sought-after collectible and is often referred to as a tribute to the dress code of the times. So give a listen to **"White Bucks And Saddle Shoes."**

 WHITE BUCKS AND SADDLE SHOES

Open your smartphone camera & scan this QR code to listen to the song.

THE BEGINNINGS OF ROCK & ROLL?
Aired in May 2020

Thanks to radio renegades like Alan Freed, who, in the 50s, stuck their necks out to play the records that their listeners wanted to hear, a new genre of music evolved – Rock & Roll ... a genre that was further legitimized with the formal opening of the Rock & Roll Hall of Fame in Cleveland, Ohio on September 2, 1995.

This genre became a part of everyone growing up in the 50s and 60s and for many of us, became an indelible part of our brand. This genre has allowed us to "rock around the clock" all these years and continues to give listeners the records they want to hear.

The record, "Rock Around The Clock" by Bill Haley and His Comets, released in 1954 via the movie *Blackboard Jungle*, would go on to become the first hit Rock & Roll single to peak at the #1 position on the pop charts. It achieved this status in July of 1955 ... and it stayed there for 8 straight weeks!

It was released as a 78 and as a 45. Back then it was commonplace for record labels to inscribe, right on the label, the type of dance that fit the music recorded – tango, two-step, or waltz, etc.

When "Rock Around The Clock" came out, the Decca label was in a bit of a quandary as to how to categorize the dance step that fit this song. But they came up with a solution - they called it a "foxtrot" and that's what appears on the label.

However, one of the burning questions today about the song is: Was "Rock Around The Clock" new and original? Some old country music fans don't think it is.

*****

"Rock Around The Clock" features a twelve-bar blues arrangement with a melody starting with three repetitions of an ascending broken chord. This is quite similar to a novelty song written and released in 1947 by the Shakespeare of country music, Hank Williams. This was Hank Williams' first charted record and it peaked at the #4 position on the country charts.

The tune itself epitomizes Williams' uncanny ability to express everyday life in a humorous way. It's about a guy who finds himself in the doghouse after coming home late at night and being barred entry by his wife.

You know, the guy probably "rocked around the clock" and subsequently, had to **"Move It On Over."**

 MOVE IT ON OVER

Open your smartphone camera & scan this QR code to listen to the song.

GREEN SHOULD'VE SIGNALED "GO"

Aired in April 2005

Rockabilly music has been credited by many as being a significant influence in the shaping of Rock & Roll. From its humble beginnings in the mid-50s, this music flourished for the balance of that decade. It was also the starting point for many artists who went on to national and international stardom – artists like Roy Orbison, Jerry Lee Lewis, Carl Perkins, the Everly Brothers, and the king himself, Elvis Presley.

Originating in the Southern United States, Rockabilly produced its share of regional stars as well. One such star was slated as a "can't miss" entertainer who, with his band, never made it nationally. They resigned themselves to being the session house band for many of Sun Records' legendary tunes.

*****

When we think of the names of other Sun Records artists who could have been and should have been national contenders, several talented names come to mind. Sonny Burgess had a booming voice like a tenor sax and a band that oozed energy, but his wild stage show just couldn't be successfully translated to records. Warren Smith had the voice, the looks, and the will to succeed, but was just too country to make the pop charts after the Rockabilly boom of 1956. Hayden Thompson huffed and puffed convincingly enough but was just too late to make it on Elvis' coattails beyond a regional level.

But the one performer who had the looks, the talent, and the ability to pull it off and didn't even come close to having a hit on Sun was Billy Riley. Though never commercially successful, Riley's Sun recordings remain landmarks of the genre.

Known to most Rockabilly fanatics as Billy Lee Riley - although the use of his middle name didn't come until the mid to late 60s - his mastery at Sun Records almost runs the whole gamut of white artists on that label. Riley's top-notch band, the Little Green Men, was the Sun house band from late 1956 on.

Covered by Sam The Sham and The Pharaohs in 1966, an original recording by Billy Lee Riley and his Little Green Men from 1956, featuring a then-unknown piano player by the name of Jerry Lee Lewis, deserves a listen – it's "**Red Hot**."

 RED HOT

Open your smartphone camera & scan this QR code to listen to the song.

WEST COAST WOMEN
Aired in April 2012

Tonight's moment in time takes us back to one of the most eclectic years in music – 1954, a year that saw established pop singers like Rosemary Clooney ("This Ole House" and "Hey There") and Perry Como ("Wanted") share #1 status with Rock & Rollers like the Crew-Cuts ("Sh-Boom") and the Chordettes ("Mr. Sandman").

R&B was beginning to go mainstream and black groups like the Crows with "Gee" were starting to gain national recognition. On the West Coast in Los Angeles an all-black girl R&B group, formed in 1953, was also getting attention.

*****

Leading the group was Shirley Gunter, who moved to Los Angeles with her parents from Coffeyville, Kansas. In 1954 Shirley and her backup group of three known as The Queens began making some noise by being the first all-black girl group to transition from R&B to Rock & Roll.

The group stayed together for three years and even had the likes of Zola Taylor performing with them prior to Zola going on to become an original member of the Platters.

Some say that the simplistic lyrics and irrepressible beat of Shirley Gunter's songs inspired future girl groups like the Bobbettes, the Marvelettes, the Cookies, the Jaynettes, and the Chantels. Although one would be hard pressed to prove with 100% accuracy that Shirley Gunter & The Queens were the first female Doo Wop group, there is no denying that their record "Oop Shoop" was the first to be written and performed, with any degree of success, by a group of young black women.

So let's go back to 1954 and revisit what female pop singers like Rosemary Clooney, Doris Day, and Jo Stafford were beginning to compete with – a new up-tempo sound epitomized by Shirley Gunter & The Queens with **"Oop Shoop."**

 OOP SHOOP

Open your smartphone camera & scan this QR code to listen to the song.

SOUNDS THE SAME

Aired in October 2009

One of the few singers ever to break out onto the Billboard Hot 100 with a #1 hit was Charlie Gracie. That record was "Butterfly," which was also a #1 hit for Andy Williams that same year – 1957.

What a start for a then 20 year old. His second hit also charted well in 1957 but met with some substantial backlash.

*****

Charlie Gracie was born in Philadelphia, Pennsylvania and appeared from time to time on *American Bandstand* from 1952-58. Short in stature at five foot four, the diminutive vocalist/guitar player did not fit the Cameo Records teen idol mode that it was promoting.

In addition to this, he sued for royalties he believed owed to him. Although his suit was settled out of court, future recordings were not that well-promoted and his record sales fell off.

One of the most controversial situations that arose in his career occurred as a result of his second release in 1957 that went Top 20. Elvis Presley's publishers made claim that Gracie's second single was too close in sound to Elvis' "Don't Be Cruel." Elvis' publishers sued for publishing rights and won.

Despite his successful touring of Great Britain on through to the 80s, it's too bad that Gracie was unable to sustain his dynamic arrival on the music scene in North America in 1957.

Some say that this talented musician deserves more recognition as a pioneer in the early days of Rock & Roll. In fact, some say he measured up to that pioneer status with his second release of 1957 in that he was simply "**Fabulous**."

 FABULOUS

Open your smartphone camera & scan this QR code to listen to the song.

THOSE TEENAGE YEARS

Aired in November 2008

One of the most successful records ever released by King Records during the early days of Rock & Roll sold over 3 million copies. Yet, its original release in 1955, which went to #5 on the Billboard Pop Charts, is rarely heard today.

*****

With the 1954 release of the movie *Blackboard Jungle* and the evolution of the "Teenager" in full swing, Rock & Roll began going mainstream. Bill Haley And His Comets were touring the nation and, as the expression goes, "the kids were diggin' this new crazy beat."

Haley rose above his competition and has become legendary. However, there were some other great bands that produced a comparable and appealing sound.

One such group was Boyd Bennett And His Rockets – certainly not a household name today but back in the mid-50s this band was a force to be reckoned with. Bennett often toured with Haley, producing a stage show that was often interpreted as "the battle of the bands."

In 1955, while under contract with King Records, Boyd Bennett and his group made their first appearance on the Billboard pop charts. Their record was a smash hit. Released in June of 1955, it made it to #5 position nationally and #1 regionally in many markets, eventually selling over 3 million copies.

Fresh off their #1 success with "Hearts Of Stone" by the Fontane Sisters, Dot Records got into the act and had the trio of girls cover Bennett's song, making it more palatable for the older generation – this worked because their version, released two months later in August of 1955, went to #3 on the charts and is heard today on oldies stations more frequently than Boyd Bennett's original version.

During the mid-50s it was not uncommon to see two or three versions of the same song out at the same time. In fact, in this particular case, Rusty Draper of "The Shifting, Whispering Sands" fame, also released a version of Boyd Bennett's tune in August for Mercury Records. As a matter of fact, it was Rusty Draper's debut on Billboard. His version made it to #18 but only lasted 4 weeks on the charts.

We probably got you guessing what the title of this record is. Many claim that it was the first Rock & Roll record created for teenage girls. Originally released on King Records by Boyd Bennett And His Rockets, its title supports this claim - "**Seventeen.**"

 SEVENTEEN

Open your smartphone camera & scan this QR code to listen to the song.

CLEAR AS MUD

Aired in February 2019

As we all know, there appears to be no definitive answer to the question, "What was the first Rock & Roll record ever made?" About the only thing that people agree on is that Rock & Roll was born out of R&B in the early 50s. From there, support for groups that "started it all" ranges from the acapella sounds of Sonny Til & The Orioles with "Crying In The Chapel" to the East Coast's Billy Ward And His Dominoes with their 1951 hit "Sixty Minute Man" to Los Angeles' Penguins with "Earth Angel" to the fabled Bill Haley And His Comets with "Rock Around The Clock."

This moment in time takes us back to 1949 and yet another record that some claim marked the beginnings of Rock & Roll.

*****

Most aficionados of Rock & Roll music side with the legendary Sam Phillips of Sun Records who claimed that an R&B song that he produced in 1951 was indeed the first Rock & Roll record. The song was written by Ike Turner and became a prototype for hundreds of other Rock & Roll records to follow.

The record was "Rocket 88" and was credited to Jackie Brenston and his Delta Cats, even though the band did not actually exist. In fact, the song was recorded by Ike Turner with his band The Kings Of Rhythm, with Brenston on a saxophone and singing lead vocals. Upon its release, Brenston was the first to comment on the record's collective appeal to both young whites and blacks.

Case closed? We don't think so. You see, back in 1949, Louis Jordan's jump blues combo put out a rearrangement of a song that was originally slated to be released by Eddie Williams and His Brown Buddies.

Louis Jordan's single was a big hit, topping the R&B charts for 12 non-consecutive weeks in late 1949. It also reached the #21 position on the national pop charts, a rare accomplishment for what was referred to as a "race record" at that time.

To add some credence to this record's rightful claim, we can't ignore Chuck Berry who was quoted as saying, "to my recollection, Louis Jordan was the first one that I heard play Rock & Roll." Ah ... leave it to Chuck to "muddy the waters."

The recording was 5 minutes and 21 seconds in length, which was longer than a standard side on a 78 record. So, it was broken into two halves, one on each side of the disc.

The song's lyrics are in the first person and describe two itinerant musicians going to a fish fry on Rampart Street in New Orleans, Louisiana. The scene becomes a wild party that is raided by the police, and the narrator ends up spending the night in jail.

Was Louis Jordan's **"Saturday Night Fish Fry"** the first Rock & Roll record? You be the judge.

 SATURDAY NIGHT FISH FRY

Open your smartphone camera & scan this QR code to listen to the song.

PAT TAKES THE RAP

Aired in March 2016

This moment in time features one of Rock & Roll's least appreciated founding fathers.

Modern rock historians have not been kind to this man. Some accuse him of being an agent in the suppression of true black music. The basis of these charges was the fact that his initial fame came as a white performer who recorded cover versions of songs first made famous by such R&B artists as Fats Domino, Little Richard, and Big Joe Turner.

However, "Shake, Rattle And Roll" did not originate with Bill Haley. Neither did "Hound Dog" originate with Elvis Presley. Jerry Lee Lewis didn't write "Whole Lotta Shakin' Goin' On" and Fats Domino's "Blueberry Hill" was an oldie going back to Gene Autry's days.

Cover versions affected white and black performers alike. Yet our featured artist was held to a different standard than many other artists, and his phenomenal fame and perennial clean-cut image made him an easy target.

*****

The fact remains that only Elvis Presley and Fats Domino sold more records than our featured artist during the golden age of Rock & Roll.

Like Elvis Presley, he was a humble country boy aspiring to croon his way to pop chart fame. Both he and Elvis gained national recognition thanks to the budding R&B-based Rock & Roll scene. Our featured artist also started out at a small label before he hit nationally, a full year before Presley, creating an opening in the mainstream for the future "king" and a score of other performers.

But to no avail. He was a marked man, saddled with being referenced as an opportunist who took advantage of black musicians and performers.

Regardless, Pat Boone sold a lot of records. And one can justifiably imagine him wondering why the music critics treated him this way, perhaps asking himself "**Why Baby Why**." As you listen to this song, ask yourself, "Should he be wondering why?"

 WHY BABY WHY

Open your smartphone camera & scan this QR code to listen to the song.

FROM
R&B
TO YOU AND ME

R&B was an integral component of Rock & Roll. However, it wasn't until 1951 that the phrase "Rock & Roll" was first coined to define the music and adopted by deejay Alan Freed, in preference to "rhythm and blues," which had a somewhat sexual connotation at the time.

Often referred to as "race records" because of their black origin and sexual suggestiveness, these tunes, far from being heard mainstream throughout North America, were limited to regional radio stations dedicated to "colored" music, but sometimes they were played on larger "white" stations by rebellious deejays like the legendary Alan Freed (Cleveland & New York), George "Hound Dog" Lorenz (Buffalo), Bill Randle (Cleveland and New York), Porky Chedwick (Pittsburgh), Jocko Henderson (Philadelphia, New York and Baltimore), Dewey Phillips (Memphis), Martha Jean "The Queen" (Memphis and Detroit), John R. Richbourg and Zenas Sears (Atlanta), Hunter Hancock (Los Angeles), and Red Robinson (Vancouver, Canada) – deejays who bucked the establishment ... an establishment who constantly told them: *You can't play that!*

Thanks to the evolution of Rock & Roll, future R&B artists and their music were able to go mainstream. Some of their stories and challenges are chronicled in the following ten moments in time.

IT WORKS FOR ME

Aired in March 2015

In June 1965, the Dave Clark Five made it onto to the North American Billboard Hot 100 for the eleventh time. This release, which featured lead singer Mike Smith's driving, gravel-like voice, would remain on the charts for 11 straight weeks and become the group's fifth Top 10 hit.

This record was actually a cover version of a 1961 hit by an R&B singer/songwriter from Louisiana.

*****

This original hit maker was born on Christmas Day in 1929. A gospel singer originally, he moved to New Orleans in his mid-teens and began recording in 1955 for Baton Records - without success.

After a brief stint with Imperial Records, he moved over to another New Orleans label, Instant Records. It was there that he began working with pianist/arranger Allen Toussaint.

In 1961, their collaboration produced a #2 Billboard pop hit that would go on to sell over one million copies. It would be the singer/songwriter's first and biggest hit despite going on to write and chart "Land Of A 1000 Dances," a great R&B tune that had no less than five cover versions, all of which charted, in a 20-year period – in order: Cannibal and The Headhunters, Thee Midniters, Wilson Pickett, Electric Indian, and the J. Geils Band.

Sadly in 1976, this singer/songwriter died suddenly from a heart attack that was believed to be triggered by alcoholism.

He will always be remembered fondly for that 1961 release that inspired the Dave Clark Five. His name was Chris Kenner and he would have been the first to tell you, **"I Like It Like That."**

 I LIKE IT LIKE THAT

Open your smartphone camera & scan this QR code to listen to the song.

THE BLIND LEADING THE WAY

Aired in May 2008

Throughout the Rock & Roll era we have been blessed with some great music by blind performers. In the early days there was Al Hibbler who had a big hit with "Unchained Melody" back in 1955. Two years later, Ray Charles made the national Billboard charts and remained on them until 1990.

In 1968, Jose Feliciano, blind from birth, hit the charts with his rendition of "Light My Fire."

However, a year prior to that, in 1967, another blind singer/guitarist made his debut nationwide thanks to his preachy R&B style that focused on the secret pursuit of love.

*****

Our black, blind artist from the South was born on January 14, 1936 in Montgomery, Alabama, and is referred to by some as the final link in a long chain of blind blues singer-guitarists - a descendant of Blind Lemon Jefferson, Blind Willie McTell, and Blind Willie Johnson, among others. Like them, he was possessed with a special vision, somewhat dark and a little frightening. In his case, love, particularly cheating love, became the great spiritual metaphor in his songs.

According to writer Brian Ward in his book, *Just My Soul Responding: Rhythm And Blues, Black Consciousness*

And Race Relations, he "virtually made a career from tales of unbridled love and illicit sex..." A classic example of this was his 80s recording, "Strokin," a song that failed to chart as it was deemed to be too risqué to be played on the radio. Ichiban Records countered this airplay rejection by placing copies of the record in jukeboxes where it became a favorite of bar patrons.

His first Top 10 record for public consumption came out in 1968 and remained on the Billboard Hot 100 for 16 straight weeks. It was a magnificent blues ballad that many lovers could relate to. You may relate as well when you **"Slip Away"** with Clarence Carter.

 SLIP AWAY

Open your smartphone camera & scan this QR code to listen to the song.

STAYING POWER

Aired in January 2016

Over the years many entertainers, both actors and musicians, have been credited with a version of the following generic quote: "It took me x number of years to become an overnight success."

One of the finest and longest performing R&B vocal groups in history can certainly lay claim to this quote as well. In fact, one of their songs, originally released in 1956, failed to become a hit until they remade it in 1969.

*****

Our featured group was formed in 1953 at Thornton Township High School in Harvey, Illinois, a suburb of Chicago. That was the beginning of a run lasting more than 60 years. What's most amazing is that they did it with nearly all the original members ... they haven't changed personnel since 1960.

In 1955 they signed with Vee-Jay Records. The following year they scored big with what has become a Doo Wop classic. Although it reached the #4 position on the R&B charts, it failed to make it on the national Billboard pop charts. However, it did establish them regionally and they began touring with their sound.

Tragedy nearly struck in 1958. On their way to a gig in Philadelphia, the group's station wagon took on a life of its own, going out of control and seriously injuring two of the group's members.

After a brief hiatus with a few of its members temporarily filling in for other groups, they re-assembled in 1960 and successfully auditioned to tour with Dinah Washington, as both her opening act and backup group. It was during that period that Johnny Carter, a former member of the Flamingos, joined the group ... it was to be the last replacement.

After Vee-Jay Records went bankrupt in 1966, the group found themselves back at Chess Records and cutting records with Cadet, a Chess subsidiary.

It was at Cadet where the group's career really started to take off. In 1967, the label assigned producer Bobby Miller and arranger Charles Stepney to handle the group. The group's first album, *There Is*, under Miller-Stepney's direction, was a smashing success, spawning no less than 4 hit singles including an expanded remake of "Stay In My Corner" that topped the R&B charts and went Top 10 on the Billboard Hot 100. Suddenly the group was bigger than they'd ever been.

In 1969 they remade their 1956 R&B recording that got them their touring gigs. This time it went national ... another Top 10 hit ... and quite an achievement for the Dells.

Oh, what a career ... and **"Oh, What A Night."**

 OH, WHAT A NIGHT

Open your smartphone camera & scan this QR code to listen to the song.

SO FINE
Aired in March 2012

Remember Old Town Records? It was one of the classic small record labels of the 50s that purportedly operated out of a cloakroom in New York's old Triboro Theatre.

The owners of Old Town Records were Sam and Hy Weiss who discovered a soulful R&B act in the late 50s. According to liner-note writer Dan Nooger, Hy Weiss paid a mere $40 to cut a record with this group ... a record that became a hit in the summer of 1959.

*****

Our featured group was made up of four members – lead vocalist Tommy Bullock, tenor Eddie Morris, baritone Sam Ingalls, and bass Preston Lane. They originally came from Newark, New Jersey but ended up in Harlem where they were discovered by Old Town Records.

In 1955 singer/songwriter Johnny Otis (of "Willie And The Hand Jive" fame) wrote a song that was released by a group called the Sheiks. Classified as strictly R&B at the time, the record had modest success regionally.

It was this song that our group from Newark recorded in 1959 on the Old Town label. The song went to #3 on the R&B charts and then crossed over to the Billboard pop charts, reaching the #11 position during a 16-week run.

Unfortunately, it was to be their only hit record and thus registered the group as a one-hit wonder despite several subsequent attempts to create R&B arrangements along the lines of Sam Cooke and Jackie Wilson.

Some critics attributed the group's lack of success to their soulful singing style being "... gritty and delightfully crude" with their rough edges possibly being too much for 60s radio.

However, there is one thing that is for sure ... when this R&B group, known as the Fiestas, crossed over from the R&B charts to the Billboard Hot 100 in June of 1959, many people used the title of their hit record to describe them ... because they were "**So Fine.**"

 SO FINE

Open your smartphone camera & scan this QR code to listen to the song.

JUST ONE CUT ABOVE

Aired in November 2012

This segment features a group from the late 60s and early 70s that is often forgotten in retrospectives of that era. The group was formed in 1968, and by the spring of the following year they had their first Top 10 hit, thanks to their talent and a retired NFL football player.

*****

The group was composed of two girls, Jessica Cleaves and Barbara Jean Love, and two guys, Floyd Butler and Harry Elston.

After polishing up their act, which was probably best described as being similar to that of the Fifth Dimension but more soulful, the group began performing in the local nightclubs in and around Los Angeles.

One thing that they did have going for them was their manager, ex-football star turned actor, Jim Brown, who got them a contract with RCA Records. Jim had moved to Los Angeles after his playing days with the Cleveland Browns. You may recall his role in *The Dirty Dozen*.

In 1969 the group's Harry Elston wrote some lyrics to the trumpet lead on a #1 R&B and pop instrumental hit that was originally recorded by trumpeter Hugh Masekela a year earlier.

The group went into the studio and created a vocalized version. The release made it onto the charts in April and remained on the R&B charts for 17 weeks, peaking at #5, and on the Billboard Hot 100 for 16 weeks, peaking at #3.

The song had a distinct soulful sound. It's no wonder that they were called the Friends Of Distinction. And it's always enjoyable "**Grazing In The Grass**" with them.

 GRAZING IN THE GRASS

Open your smartphone camera & scan this QR code to listen to the song.

HE WAS COOL WITH IT

Aired in June 2018

This moment in time features an American R&B singer/songwriter and arranger who has been described as "one of the most interesting obscure figures of 60s soul music."

Although he only made the North American charts three times in the late 60s, he did it twice with the same record.

***** *

Born in 1941 in the Bronx in New York, this artist started out as a songwriter and arranger. In fact, his first songwriting credit came in 1957 at the age of 16 when he co-wrote the song "The Lord Will Understand (And Say 'Well Done')." It ended up on the B side of "Got A Date With An Angel," a 1957 single by the legendary Billy Williams.

The song was banned by the BBC in Britain for "religious overtones," ... which is ironic as the artist would eventually move to England permanently in 1969.

In 1964 the artist moved on to Redbird Records and co-wrote "It's Easier To Cry" which ended up on the B side of the Shangri-La's first hit, "Remember (Walkin' In The Sand)."

As a singer he finally made the scene in 1966 with a song

he co-wrote with Pierre Tubbs, a song that suited his ability to belt out a tune.

It made the Billboard Hot 100 in both 1966 and 1969 and was one of the first R&B hit singles to have been originally recorded in England.

His singing style is similar to David Clayton Thomas of Blood, Sweat And Tears.

Born Jerome Louis Jackson, he is better known as J. J. Jackson. If you asked him if he was disappointed with his lack of notoriety in North America, he would just shrug his shoulders and say, "**But It's Alright.**"

 BUT IT'S ALRIGHT

Open your smartphone camera & scan this QR code to listen to the song.

THE STING REMAINS

Aired in April 2020

This moment in time focuses on a charismatic, black R&B artist who grew up in Chicago and went on to become one of the most prominent artists in the early days of Rock & Roll, despite having many of her hits covered by white vocalists.

*****

Born Delores Williams on November 11, 1929, this artist first recorded as "Little Miss Sharecropper" in 1949. She was blessed with a sound that was a mixture of sophistication and down-to-earth power reminiscent to that of the legendary Bessie Smith, with whom Williams later recorded a tribute album prior to leaving the Atlantic Records label in 1964.

She signed on with Atlantic Records in 1953, and under a new stage name, went on to have 20 R&B releases that crossed over to the national pop charts from 1955 to 1966 – her last charted release was a duet with Jackie Wilson ("Think Twice") on the Brunswick label.

Her most successful recording came out in December of 1958 and went to the #6 position, remaining on the charts for 21 straight weeks. The record was "I Cried A Tear."

Oddly enough, today when her name is mentioned, this is not the record that comes to mind.

What does come to mind are two of her earlier mid-50s releases, "Jim Dandy" and "Tweedlee Dee." They both made it onto the national charts but did not get as much airplay as the cover versions released by her white female counterparts.

"Jim Dandy," which is often heard today, went to #17 on the national pop charts and #1 on the R&B charts.

In the case of "Tweedlee Dee," her breakout record, it went to a respectable #14 on the pop charts – however, it was covered by white recording star, Georgia Gibbs, whose version went to #2 on the same charts.

Unlike many other African-American artists of that time, Williams protested and filed suit, claiming that her own interpretation of "Tweedlee Dee" constituted a copyrightable arrangement. Her suit was unsuccessful.

Story has it that, upon heading off on an Australian tour, Williams bought herself some flight insurance and enclosed it with a letter that she mailed to Gibbs. The stinging letter stated that Gibbs might need the insurance money in case something happened to Williams while she was on tour and Gibbs wouldn't have any more of her material to copy.

In 1960, Williams, better known to us as LaVern Baker, gave a little more sting with the charted recording and lost treasure, "**Bumble Bee**."

 BUMBLE BEE

Open your smartphone camera & scan this QR code to listen to the song.

BALLADS STILL HAVE A PLACE

Aired in September 2018

This moment in time features an R&B group originally from New Jersey that was around for over 14 years before making it to #1 on both the R&B charts and the Billboard Hot 100.

*****

The group was formed in 1962 and consisted of five members. Its first single was "For The Very First Time" and was released in 1964 on Carnival Records.

The group continued to record successfully with compositions written by members of the group. By the time 1975 rolled around, the group had made it onto the Billboard Hot 100 nine times and had been firmly entrenched at Columbia Records ... somewhat remarkable since tragedy had struck with the loss of their lead singer, George Smith, in 1970 from a brain tumor.

Upon Smith's passing, the group decided to approach another artist to replace him. This singer was Gerald Alston who had previously turned down their invitation to join them. This time, he accepted. For trivia buffs, Gerald Alston is the nephew of Shirley Alston-Reeves, the lead singer of the Shirelles.

It was with Gerald Alston as the lead that the group hit pay dirt in 1976, thanks to a song written by Blue Lovett and arranged/co-produced by Bobby Martin, a former member of the MFSB band of session musicians. The record quickly soared to the #1 position on both the Billboard pop and R&B charts in July of that year.

What is amazing about this song is that it is yet another reminder that there is always room on the charts for a good ballad – no matter what music genre seems to be trending. This was certainly a great ballad.

Listening to this song can be bittersweet as four members of this group, the Manhattans, have passed on. About all we can do is just "**Kiss And Say Goodbye**."

 KISS AND SAY GOODBYE

Open your smartphone camera & scan this QR code to listen to the song.

SHE HAD RHYTHM

Aired in December 2011

In November of 2006 we lost a great pioneering singer/ songwriter who had achieved national acceptance in bringing a pop music style to the R&B music published by Atlantic Records in the 50s and 60s.

Known as "Miss Rhythm," the title of her 1995 autobiography, she was inspired by artists such as Sarah Vaughan, Billie Holiday, and Dinah Washington.

She crossed over to the national Billboard pop charts from the R&B charts in 1957. Her second entry on the charts in 1958 proved to be her most successful, even though it is rarely heard today.

*****

This pop and R&B singer/songwriter extraordinaire hailed from Portsmouth, Virginia. In 1945 at the age of 17, she ran away from home along with trumpeter Jimmy Brown, whom she married, to pursue a career singing in bars and nightclubs.

She soon found herself in New York with an Atlantic Records' contract. In 1950 she recorded an upbeat number, "Teardrops From My Eyes," which became a Billboard #1 R&B hit for 11 weeks. The hit earned her the nickname Miss Rhythm, and within a few months she became the acknowledged Queen of R&B.

In 1957 she released "Lucky Lips," the first of seven R&B records to cross over to the pop charts. This was the same song that England's Cliff Richard cut a version of and had success with in 1963.

Her follow-up tune in 1958 for Atlantic Records went to #7 on the R&B charts and a respectable #24 on the pop charts.

This singer/songwriter, who would go on to become a record producer, composer, and actress, was born Ruth Weston. We know this music legend better as Ruth Brown. Thanks to her efforts, Atlantic Records, like Yankee Stadium, became known as "the house that Ruth built."

Miss Rhythm aka Ruth Brown was indeed a force, and her energy is definitely depicted in this 1958 crossover release, "**This Little Girl's Gone Rockin'.**"

THIS LITTLE GIRL'S GONE ROCKIN'

Open your smartphone camera & scan this QR code to listen to the song.

BRING IT ON

Aired in January 2006

Probably one of the greatest artists to ever hit the Billboard charts was the late, great Sam Cooke. Ironically, his only number #1 hit was his first charted record in 1957, the classic "You Send Me."

On many of his subsequent recordings, Cooke was backed by popular orchestras led by the likes of Bumps Blackwell, Don Ralke, and Sammy Lowe, to name a few.

However, on a double-sided hit released in the spring of 1962, Cooke was accompanied by a singer whose voice subsequently became as distinctive and instantly recognizable as any in music.

*****

By the spring of 1962, Cooke had made it onto the Billboard charts 22 times with two of his recordings going Top 10 ("Chain Gang" went to #2 in 1960 and "Twistin' The Night Away" made it to the #9 position in February of 1962).

Still on a roll, Cooke had double success with the release of "Bring It On Home To Me" and "Having A Party" (which was on the B side). What was unique about these tunes was the vocal sound of the backup singer, a member of Cooke's group, the Travelers.

This proved to be the beginning of the backup artist's solo career, a career that spanned over 25 years and included such charted classics as "You'll Never Find Another Love Like Mine" and "Lady Love."

Yes, the man accompanying Sam Cooke on two of his 1962 releases was none other than Lou Rawls who sadly passed away in January 2006 at the age of 72 ... the man with a voice that one critic called "sweet as sugar, soft as velvet, strong as steel, smooth as butter."

With their gospel heritage showing, Sam Cooke and Lou Rawls gave it their all with "**Bring It On Home To Me.**"

Open your smartphone camera & scan this QR code to listen to the song.

STREET CORNER

HARMONY

Street corner harmony for the most part was an urban phenomenon. Today, it is often associated with the term "Doo Wop." However, truth be known, the term "Doo Wop" was not originally coined until the 1970s, evolving from the meaningless background sounds and lyrics used by vocal groups during the 50s and early 60s.

It has been conservatively estimated that throughout this era there were hundreds of groups on the street corners and in the subways of New York alone, singing and harmonizing without the accompaniment of musical instruments. The goal for these acapella groups was to create a unique sound and be discovered so they could make a record that would be played on the radio. The fact that girls would take notice of them was an added bonus for the predominantly male groups.

Many of these groups did not last long. However, many were able to obtain their "fifteen minutes of fame" before they broke up and went into obscurity. Although the groups disappeared, their music hasn't and this style of music and the tunes from this early era of Rock & Roll remain with us today.

The following ten segments are representative of the style of this music and the trials and tribulations of these young performers. They didn't make much money, but they sure had their moment in time.

FROM A STREET IN THE BRONX

Aired in July 2011

When it comes to staying power, a tip of the hat goes out to a 50s vocal harmony group named after a street in the Bronx in New York City.

After losing their lead singer who chose a solo career, the group honed their early harmonies and became a trio. It paid off for them with a huge regional hit that also made it to the 18th position on the national charts in 1961.

Twenty years later, after an 18-year absence, they made it onto the Billboard charts again.

*****

The group originally featured four Italian teenagers who soon became the pride of the Bronx in the late 50s. They were originally known as Dion and The Belmonts with the "Belmont" moniker inspired by a Belmont Avenue street sign in the Bronx.

In a two-year period, from 1958 to 1960, the group charted nine times including such original classics as "I Wonder Why," "A Teenager In Love," and a beautiful remake of "Where Or When."

Dion decided to leave the group in the summer of 1960. One year later, he had 5 charted singles including "Runaround Sue" that went to #1.

With their harmonies intact, the Belmonts released their version of an up-tempo regional hit originally performed by Norman Fox & The Rob-Roys in 1957. The Belmonts' version went national in 1961 and reached the 18th position on the Billboard charts.

The group would go on to chart 5 more times in the next 2 years.

From time to time, over the next 2 decades, the group would unite with Dion, the highlight being their famous performance at Madison Square Garden on June 2, 1972.

As the 70s came to a close, having another record make the charts appeared remote. That was until Freddie Cannon came along. Cannon hadn't had a hit since "The Dedication Song" in 1966.

He teamed up with the Belmonts in 1981 and together they released "Let's Put The Fun Back In Rock 'N' Roll."

Now that's staying power.

We don't know what possessed them to do it but perhaps if we reflect upon their 1961 hit, the Belmonts might **"Tell Me Why."**

TELL ME WHY

Open your smartphone camera & scan this QR code to listen to the song.

NO! NO! NO!

Aired in December 2020

One gimmick that was used by many artists and pro-ducers that resulted in "one-hit wonder" status on the Billboard Hot 100 was that of creating a "sound-alike." Two good examples of this, from 1965, are the Knicker-bockers and a group called The Silkie who had success by sounding like the Beatles.

The New Jersey-based Knickerbockers did it with "Lies" (#20) and The Silkie did it with "You've Got To Hide Your Love Away" (#10), a song from the Beatles' movie *Help*. It should also be noted that the Beatles contributed musical accompaniment and production assistance on The Silkie Top 10 recording.

Prior to the Beatles there were other groups and artists that were emulated by their peers. When it came to singing acapella, the adage was, "if you can't establish your own unique blend of harmony, then sound like someone else who was successful."

*****

During the vocal group harmony craze of the 50s and its resurgence in the early 60s, it seemed that every street corner in New York had a group of teenagers honing their acapella skills with the hopes that they would be discovered. Most weren't discovered or had some regional success and then disbanded.

In 1957 five guys from Queens, New York formed an R&B group. One of the members, Bud Johnson, was the son of the famous bandleader Buddy Johnson who consented to arrange the group's session.

However, it wasn't until the summer of 1961 during the acapella resurgence that the group finally made the Billboard pop charts, peaking at the modest 41st position.

What has endured for them is the fact that their recorded single has become a collector's item, valued at more than $50. Many say that it has a lot to do with their sound for they are often mistaken for Frankie Lymon And The Teenagers. In fact, as you listen to this song by the Chanters, you may recall the tune "I'm Not A Juvenile Delinquent" that Frankie Lymon And The Teenagers originally recorded and also performed in the Alan Freed movie, *Rock, Rock, Rock.*

This makes you wonder how many times that the Chanters, when asked if they were indeed Frankie Lymon And The Teenagers, had to reply, "**No, No, No**."

 NO, NO, NO

Open your smartphone camera & scan this QR code to listen to the song.

AMAZING
Aired in March 2020

In 1955, an R&B vocal group formed at a Manhattan junior high school was about as integrated as a group could get, composed of four men (two blacks, a Puerto Rican, and an Italian) and one black female. In 1956 another Italian joined the group that eventually pared down to a four-man quartet by 1958.

The group found the New York City subway system the perfect venue to hone their sound.

*****

It was during one of their subway sessions in 1957 that a woman stood up and handed the group a business card reading "Al Browne And Orchestra." Al Browne was a well-known arranger who backed up the Heartbeats and other acts at the time. And that woman on the subway? ... Mrs. Al Browne.

The group recorded with Browne in June of 1957 and would go on to grace the Billboard Hot 100 ten times in a 3-year span.

Their biggest hit went to #2 on the charts in 1959, thanks to deejays Alan Freed and Dick Clark promoting the B side of a November 1958 release. That record was "16 Candles."

The group, of course, was the Crests, which featured the incomparable voice of Johnny Maestro.

By early 1960, there was mounting pressure on the group from their Coed Record label to have Johnny Maestro go solo. Ironically, this came to a head after the release of "Trouble In Paradise."

Maestro did go on his own but was only a regional success and the Crests failed to have another charted record.

Maestro eventually hooked up with the Del-Satins and a 7-piece band known as the Rhythm Method to form the Brooklyn Bridge (of "The Worst That Could Happen" fame).

Some speculate that the Crests' last 2 singles in 1960 were not promoted as heavily because of Maestro's pending departure.

Still, the Crests had a great run, and like the title of their last charted song, you could say this about that run: **"Isn't It Amazing."**

 ISN'T IT AMAZING

Open your smartphone camera & scan this QR code to listen to the song.

SLEEP SINGERS

Aired in May 2005

Have you ever asked yourself what certain recordings by Dee Clark, the Cascades and Lou Christie have in common? Maybe not.

However, if you did some quick research you would soon come up with the fact that they all had a hit record that dealt with rain – Dee Clark had "Raindrops" in 1961, the Cascades had the classic ballad "Rhythm Of The Rain" in 1963, and Lou Christie, in 1966, put out the controversial, for then, "Rhapsody In The Rain."

But they had something else in common. In the production of these records, you will hear the sound of rain.

Not to be outdone, a vocal harmony group in the early 60s also simulated a sound in their hit record – and it wasn't rain ... it was a bowling alley!

* * * * *

When reflecting on their success in music, many acapella groups and their fans will be quick to point out the importance of creating a unique sound.

The complementing of four-part harmonies with background sounds and sound effects soon became an integral part in production recording. Such was the case for the Devotions, originally a 6-man group who came out of the Astoria, Queens section of New York City in 1960.

In 1961 the Devotions released their cover version of the standard "For Sentimental Reasons" on Delta Records. Unfortunately for them, the Cleftones released the same record a few weeks later and it became a substantial hit. Realizing this, Delta Records began promoting the B side of the Devotions' recording. Unfortunately again, the record did nothing.

Soon afterwards Delta sold the master to Roulette Records who also did nothing with it until 1964 when they released it as a cut on an "oldies" album. After the song started receiving airplay, Roulette released it as a single – it sold more than 10,000 copies in a week and eventually went Top 40 on the national charts.

A lot of the credit for its success was given to its unusual "bowling alley" opening, something that still captures fans of the group to this day. Considered one of the classics of urban street corner harmony, this song by the Devotions tells quite the story about "**Rip Van Winkle.**"

 RIP VAN WINKLE

Open your smartphone camera & scan this QR code to listen to the song.

THE CONEY ISLAND EXPERIENCE
Aired in February 2010

In the early days of Rock & Roll, some artists were inspired by others and some were inspired by their surroundings. In the case of an early 60s vocal group from the Bronx in New York City, it was a combination of both.

*****

In the early 60s, the Bronx was a hotbed for vocal groups. New acts were greatly encouraged by more established groups like Dion and The Belmonts, Nino & the Ebb Tides, and the Regents (of "Barbara Ann" fame).

One such fortunate vocal group was one of the few all-white sextets, originally formed as the Premiers in 1960.

In 1961, with a name change in place, the group recorded 2 cuts that were released back to back on Blast Records. The A side was an up-tempo version of the Cleftones "You Baby You" that originally charted in 1956 on Gee Records. Although preferred today by many over the Cleftones' version, the 1961 release went nowhere.

In April 1962 "You Baby You" was released again and got some traction regionally. However, it was the B side that started to get serious airplay this time around.

The B side was inspired by Lili Loftus, a hostess at Astroland in Coney Island. New York disc jockeys began playing the record in conjunction with bathing suit contests at that famous amusement park.

By the fall of 1962, the record started receiving unpromoted national airplay and rose to a respectable 51st position on the Billboard charts by late November of that year.

The group itself was flying high and doing shows with New York deejay Cousin Brucie and playing at the Palisades Amusement Park in New Jersey.

With original lead singer John Kuse, the group, now a quartet, is still going strong today and living up to their name, the Excellents, while continuing to sing about their **"Coney Island Baby."**

 CONEY ISLAND BABY

Open your smartphone camera & scan this QR code to listen to the song.

THE OTHER BROTHER

Aired in February 2009

In October of 2008 we were all saddened by the death of Joe Stubbs, the great lead singer of the Four Tops. His memory and his songs will live on forever.

Ten years prior to that, in 1998, Levi lost his younger brother, Joe Stubbs, to cancer at the age of 57.

Perhaps not as identifiable as Levi, Joe had a remarkable career that spanned four decades. He first gained prominence in 1959 with a group that was originally conceived in the mid-50s by Eddie Floyd who went on to a successful solo career, which included his 1966 number one R&B hit, "Knock On Wood."

*****

Although Eddie Floyd was the recognized lead singer of the group from its inception in 1955 through to 1961, it was Joe Stubbs who sang the lead on the group's first and biggest hit ever to make the Billboard charts.

Joe subsequently left the group in 1960 and hooked up with the Contours and the Originals. After his Motown years, Joe enjoyed his greatest success while singing lead for the soul group, 100 Proof Aged In Soul. In 1970 they scored big with "Somebody's Been Sleeping," which went to the #8 on the Billboard Hot 100 and remained on the charts for 14 straight weeks.

In the mid-90s, Joe was promoted as a solo artist and released an album, *The Best Of Joe Stubbs* that met with critical acclaim. He was a vibrant, spirited tenor who is best summed up by the title of the song he sang lead on for the Falcons in 1959 ... **"You're So Fine."**

Epilogue: For you trivia buffs, in 1961 the Falcons replaced lead singer Eddie Floyd with a young energetic performer by the name of Wilson Pickett!

 YOU'RE SO FINE

Open your smartphone camera & scan this QR code to listen to the song.

THE FAB FIVE
Aired in October 2007

In 1956 in New Haven, Connecticut, a new group called the Five Satins was formed by singer/songwriter Fred Parris. While stationed with the army in Japan, Parris wrote the group's greatest hit, "In The Still Of The Nite," on which he sang lead. It was first released on Standord, a small Connecticut label. Today a mint copy of that original release would fetch well over $1,000.

The song was subsequently picked up by Ember Records of New York. Ironically, that tune was the B side of the record, a record that would go on to earn the distinction of being the only record ever to make it on to the Billboard Hot 100 on 3 separate occasions in the same version by the same group – it reached the 24th position in 1956; the 81st position in 1960; and, the 99th position in 1961.

The group's second biggest hit became a favorite of young lovers in 1957. However, it was Bill Baker, not Fred Parris, who sang lead on this release.

*****

In 1982 in a medley entitled "Memories Of Days Gone By," "In The Still Of The Nite" was featured along with "Sixteen Candles" (Crests), "Earth Angel" (Penguins), "Only You" (Platters), "A Thousand Miles Away" (Heartbeats), "Tears On My Pillow" (Little Anthony And The

Imperials), and "Since I Don't Have You" (Skyliners). It was performed under the banner Fred Parris & The Five Satins.

However, in 1957, with Bill Baker singing lead, the group had its second biggest hit. Why Bill Baker? Simple ... Parris was in the army! He rejoined the group, replacing Baker, in January of 1958.

This Five Satins' 1957 recording was often heard at weddings during the late 50s. It was also rediscovered in the classic nostalgic movie *American Graffiti* (1973), being introduced by the incomparable Wolfman Jack. The song ... **"To The Aisle."**

 TO THE AISLE

Open your smartphone camera & scan this QR code to listen to the song.

HE'S HEAVY & HE'S MY BROTHER

Aired in September 2008

As we moved into the late 50s, the signature sound of Rock & Roll vocal groups was a high tenor lead that was applied to both up-tempo songs and ballads. Groups like the Capris with "There's A Moon Out Tonight" were a classic example.

In late 1956, a young boy who went by the name of Louie decided that he would follow in his older brother's footsteps and take the tenor lead in his own group.

✶✶✶✶✶

As the story goes, Louie and his new-formed group soon met backstage at the Apollo Theatre with record producer Bobby Robinson while his older brother was performing on stage with his group. Louie and his group inked a 2-year deal that night and began recording on Fury Records in January 1957.

The group went on to have several regional hits and was well received on the East Coast. However, Louie and his group never achieved the national recognition bestowed on his older brother, despite memorable stage performances, catchy tunes, and beautiful harmonies.

Although the group did go on to appear in the movie *Jamboree*, probably one of Louie's most memorable and satisfying moments was performing alongside his brother in 1957 at the New York Paramount where both brothers and their respective groups brought down the house during an Alan Freed show.

That older brother was Frankie Lymon, and his group, the Teenagers.

They were trendsetters in the early days of Rock & Roll and were the benchmark that hundreds of vocal harmony groups aspired to in assessing their capabilities and garnering public recognition.

On stage, Louie and his group were better known as Lewis Lymon And The Teenchords ... and it was on stage that Louie, via his first Fury Record release, proclaimed, **"I'm So Happy."**

 I'M SO HAPPY

Open your smartphone camera & scan this QR code to listen to the song.

FROM JAZZ TO ROCK & ROLL

Aired in May 2005

Johnny Carson, the famous talk show host, was once quoted as saying, "There are only nine original jokes in the world ... all the others are just variations."

When it comes to street corner harmony, some people have made the same claim. Many of the successes in this offshoot of Rock & Roll came as a result of revitalizing, rearranging, or spicing up music first released in the 30s and 40s.

*****

By the time the 60s rolled around, almost every street corner and subway platform in New York City featured a group of teenagers singing acapella in four-part harmony. They all knew that the keys for success were creating a unique sound, being consistent, and getting discovered.

To do this, many groups turned to standard songs from the 30s and 40s. The Flamingos found success with the standard, "I Only Have Eyes For You," the Platters followed suit with "Smoke Gets In Your Eyes," and the Classics did a beautiful rendition of "Till Then."

Other groups like the Cleftones with "Heart & Soul," Frankie Lymon with "Goody, Goody," and the Marcels with "Blue Moon" took these standards and created up-tempo arrangements that "Teenage America" embraced. These performers also raised a few eyebrows with some of the older generation who felt it was sacrilegious to mess with melodic hits from the past.

The above-mentioned tunes and groups were very successful in becoming nationally recognized. However, many successes were only regional, the Northeastern part of the United States being the hotbed.

One regionally successful group from 1961 remembers winning Record of the Night and then Record of the Week on deejay Murray The K's *Swingin' Soiree*, beating out "The Wanderer" by Dion.

However, what has proved more interesting over time is the speculation about what might have happened had this group, the Quotations, recorded for a record label other than Verve.

The first Rock & Roll group to record on Verve, a strictly jazz label until this group came along, The Quotations had a distinctive sound and talent for putting their own special spin on songs that had been previously recorded and considered to be standards. The unique bass riffs and high tenor parts plus their creative backgrounds remain the trademark of this group.

Would they have enjoyed a string of hits with another label? You be the judge – sit back, listen, and use your **"Imagination."**

IMAGINATION

Open your smartphone camera & scan this QR code to listen to the song.

UNDER THE "B"

Aired in February 2009

In the early days of Rock & Roll, it was often a crap shoot as to which side of a record was going to attract the public's attention. Thank goodness the deejays of that era didn't always listen to the record execs and promoters as to what was a "can't-miss hit."

In 1954 a number of deejays in Los Angeles, including Johnny Otis (of "Willie And The Hand Jive" fame), began playing the B side of a record that was destined to become a Rock & Roll classic and a Valentine's Day favorite.

*****

In 1954 Cleve Duncan, a student at Freemont High in Los Angeles, decided to form a singing group. He met up with Curtis Williams, who had co-written a song with Jesse Belvin, who would go on to release "Goodnight My Love" in 1956. Reportedly, Williams' co-writing was inspired by the love for his wife, Marlene.

Duncan liked the song and recruited Dexter Tisby for the group. Williams reciprocated by bringing Bruce Tate into the fold. They called themselves the Penguins, a name inspired by Willie the Penguin who appeared on the packages of Kool cigarettes.

Williams' song about his girlfriend was recorded on the B side with "Hey Senorita" featured on the A side.

"Hey Senorita" was nice but didn't cut it with the dee-jays in LA, who consistently played the flipside. Thanks to them, the B side became one of the first R&B hits to make it on the Billboard pop charts nationally. It was released in November of 1954 and stayed on the charts for 15 weeks, peaking at the #8 position.

This tune has become one of the all-time Rock & Roll classics. It is one of the most played and biggest selling records ever. An original 45 of this cool Penguin ballad on the Dootone label is worth a few hundred dollars today. If you are fortunate to have a copy for sale, any record collector would consider you an **"Earth Angel."**

 EARTH ANGEL

Open your smartphone camera & scan this QR code to listen to the song.

North American vocal groups and bands flourished in the late 50s, 60s, and 70s, being both challenged and inspired by their British counterparts during the latter two decades.

Parallel with this was the song writing. Lyrics matured with the music, evolving from simple words and phrases that put a smile on your face to thought-provoking messages. Stage performances and TV appearances contributed to group recognition and their "brand," a word many of us were introduced to for the first time.

The following ten segments run the gamut from "having a good beat and you can dance to it" to using music as a platform to make a statement about life and our culture.

A SONG OF MARRIAGE

Aired in November 2015

A recent visit to the Rock & Roll Hall Of Fame in Cleveland led to the discovery of a very significant date for one of the most memorable records to come out of the early days of Rock & Roll.

The date in question was June 28, 1957, a date that was the catalyst for a story about this record that will give you goose bumps.

*****

Does the name Jerome Felder mean anything to you? Probably not. How about his pen name ... Doc Pomus? A little more familiar?

Doc Pomus was an American blues singer and prolific songwriter who was featured in the 2012 documentary *A.K.A. Doc Pomus*. He is best known as a lyricist and composer who teamed up with Mort Shuman to write such Rock & Roll and pop classics as "A Teenager In Love," "Hushabye," "This Magic Moment," "Turn Me Loose," "Sweets For My Sweet," "Go Jimmy Go," "Little Sister," "Can't Get Used To Losing You," "Suspicion," "Surrender," and "(Marie's The Name) His Latest Flame."

Before devoting his time fully to songwriting, he performed as a blues singer and actually recorded around 40 songs during the 40s and 50s for record companies like Chess, Apollo, and Gotham.

According to Pomus, more often than not, he was the only Caucasian in the clubs. And, as a Jew and a polio victim, he felt a special underdog kinship with African Americans, while in turn the audiences both respected his courage and were impressed with his talent.

He had contracted polio as a young boy and walked with crutches. Later on in life he was confined to a wheelchair.

On June 28, 1957, he married Broadway actress and dancer Willi Burke. During the wedding reception, while his new bride was cavorting on the dance floor, Pomus wrote a song on a wedding invitation, a song that would become a #1 hit for the Drifters in 1960.

That wedding invitation with the handwritten lyrics is on display at the Rock & Roll Hall Of Fame in Cleveland.

As to the song, it outlines Pomus' perspective on the evening: he tells his wife to have fun dancing while reminding her who will be taking her home. He also insisted that she "**Save The Last Dance For Me**."

SAVE THE LAST DANCE FOR ME

Open your smartphone camera & scan this QR code to listen to the song.

ONE OF THE FIRST MUSIC VIDEOS

Aired in May 2001

Over the years Rock & Roll has introduced some of the most unique and remarkable voices to the music scene. The girl groups of the 50s and 60s definitely included some of these.

A few that come to mind are Arlene Smith of the Chantels ("Maybe"), Darlene Love who sang lead on the Crystals' 1962 smash hit "He's A Rebel," and, of course, Diana Ross of the Supremes.

However, if you asked Ellie Greenwich, the famous 60s singer/songwriter who penned a number of hits with former husband Jeff Barry, she would tell you that one of the most natural and captivating voices of the 60s music scene belonged to a girl by the name of Brenda Reid.

*****

Brenda Reid was born and raised in Jamaica, New York. As a high school junior in 1962 she sang with classmates Carol Johnson and Lillian Walker. Late in 1962, Herb Rooney joined the girls after his group had disbanded. A little older than the girls, Herb worked as a record producer.

The group soon landed a recording contract with United Artists and recorded a Bert Russell song that reached the #4 position on the Billboard Hot 100 in 1963, the same year that the girls graduated.

Reid sang lead on this hit tune, a tune whose success Ellie Greenwich attributes to Reid's unique, upbeat style.

On occasion you can see Brenda Reid and the rest of the group performing the tune on MTV when they flash back to the early years. Back in 1963, someone had the presence of mind to film them singing their hit song - in a zoo, no less! – thus making it one of the first music videos.

Brenda Reid with Carol, Lillian, and Herb, better known as the Exciters, empowered teenage girls with their smash 1963 hit, "**Tell Him**."

Open your smartphone camera & scan this QR code to listen to the song.

CATCH YOU ON THE FLIPSIDE

Aired in January 2015

Back in the day you may have been at a party and heard a record that just made you get up on your feet and dance like there was no tomorrow. This moment in time falls into that category.

Ironically, this song was deemed to be a non-hit, destined to never see the light of day, and so was released on the B side of a 45 that came out in 1965.

Thanks to a radio station's willingness to play this B side since the A side had failed miserably, a group from the Southern United States ended up with a Top 10 hit.

*****

In the summer of 1963, a seven-man group was formed in Memphis, Tennessee. Over the course of the next year and a half, they came in third place in the Mid-South Fair talent competition. Their steady improvement earned them an appearance on *Ted Mack's Amateur Hour*, and subsequently won them top honors at the Memphis Battle Of The Bands.

While cutting their second record, they decided that the flipside would be a cover of a song originally done by the Avantis, a group they had befriended and toured with.

The lead vocals were performed by the group leader, Larry Raspberry, who later said, "It was the first time I had sung this song ... it was done for the flipside, so there was nothing to be lost with my not having a good voice."

This flipside soared to the #4 position on the Billboard charts in the fall of 1965.

The group went on to tour and opened for Jerry Lee Lewis, the Beach Boys, and Paul Revere And The Raiders. They also performed on television shows including *Shindig*, *American Bandstand* twice, and *Where The Action Is*.

The group was known as the Gentrys. Their 1965 hit record was done in one take but was only one minute and thirty seconds long – too short even for a B side, so they taped the beginning over and stuck it at the end, adding a pause in between which contributed to the song's uniqueness. It also had an added bonus as it encouraged their fans to "**Keep On Dancing**."

Epilogue: A note for wrestling fans: one of the other original members of the Gentrys, Jimmy Hart, went on to become a successful and flamboyant wrestling manager with the World Wrestling Federation. Fittingly, he went by the moniker "The Mouth of the South."

 KEEP ON DANCING

Open your smartphone camera & scan this QR code to listen to the song.

THE KEY INGREDIENT

Aired in April 2018

This moment in time features a trio formed in 1964 in Harlem. Eight years and two name changes later, the group made it to the Top 10 on both the pop and R&B charts.

*****

The group, originally known as the Poets, made their first recordings for Leiber and Stoller's Red Bird label. Soon after, they changed their name to the Insiders and signed with RCA Records. In 1968, the last name change occurred, a name that was inspired by wording on a Coca-Cola bottle.

Hooking up with producer Bert DeCoteaux proved to be very timely. Thanks to DeCoteaux's sense of where soul music was heading, the group made it to the Top 30 on the R&B charts for the first time in 1970 with "You've Been My Inspiration," a song which was the first of five releases to cross over to the Billboard Hot 100. All this occurred within fifteen months.

Unfortunately, tragedy struck the group in 1971 when lead singer Don McPherson died unexpectedly from leukemia. Surviving members Tony Silvester and Luther Simmons re-grouped with a new lead singer who had served as a backing vocalist on some of their previous recordings and had filled in on tour during McPherson's brief illness.

That new lead singer was Cuba Gooding Sr., the father of future Academy Award winner Cuba Gooding Jr. His first release with the group, which was their biggest success, was a smash hit reaching #2 on the R&B charts and #3 on the Billboard Hot 100, selling over a million copies.

Like the group's Coca-Cola inspired name, he proved to be the Main Ingredient for "**Everybody Plays The Fool.**"

Epilogue: For you trivia buffs, Bert DeCoteaux and Main Ingredient member, Tony Silvester, would go on to produce "Supernatural Thing – Part I, Part II" for Ben E. King with Part I topping the R&B charts and peaking at the #5 position on the Billboard Hot 100 in 1975.

 EVERYBODY PLAYS THE FOOL

Open your smartphone camera & scan this QR code to listen to the song.

LIVING THE DREAM
Aired in December 2010

No one can deny the upbeat nature of many Rock & Roll records, especially those from the early 60s. Things were light and simple and we had yet to be introduced on a grand scale to the likes of Bob Dylan.

One lesser-known group from the Philadelphia area, who excelled at lifting up the spirits of teenagers, finally hit it big nationally in the summer of 1962.

*****

In 1960 this group entered a recording studios as the Premiers and came out known as the Versatiles after recording "I'll Whisper In Your Ear" and "Lundee Dundee" on the B side. This record, issued on Ro-Cal Records, has become a Doo Wop collector's item.

Two years later, the five-member group, which was composed of four boys and one girl, transformed from an R&B group to a pop group along the lines of the Four Seasons. The transformation also included another name change.

The first and most successful of their three charted records was released in August of 1962 and went to #22 on the Billboard charts, remaining on the charts for 11 straight weeks.

What is little known about this song is that the high lead voice on the song is not that of female member Idella

Morris, but actually that of Ricky Cordo, an unusually high tenor.

The group's new name was the Majors. Fortunately for them, they got to live and sing about their **"Wonderful Dream."**

 WONDERFUL DREAM

Open your smartphone camera & scan this QR code to listen to the song.

ALL ABOARD

Aired in October 2008

In the mid to late 60s we were introduced to "bubble-gum music," which is described in Wikipedia as "an upbeat sound that is considered to be disposable, contrived, or marketed for children and adolescents." One of the first groups to make it in this genre was the Music Explosion, a pop rock group that had a huge hit with "A Little Bit O' Soul," which went to #2 in the spring of 1967.

The producers of this Ohio group, Jerry Kasenetz and Jeff Katz, would go on to discover and produce records for similar groups like the 1910 Fruitgum Company and the Ohio Express.

On many of the Ohio Express hits, Joey Levine sang lead. Yet Levine rarely toured with the group. In fact, most of their hits were recorded by studio musicians in New York.

Even more outlandish was how their breakout record made it onto the charts.

****

The Ohio Express came from Mansfield, Ohio but were originally known as Sir Timothy & the Royals. Once discovered by Kasenetz and Katz, they changed their name to be more American sounding.

To get the group off and running, they took an unsuccessful single originally performed by another group, Rare Breed, and re-released it on the Cameo-Parkway label unchanged, except with the Ohio Express' name on it. It remained on the charts for 12 straight weeks in the fall of 1967, peaking at the 29th position.

With Cameo-Parkway in decline, Kasenetz and Katz moved over to Buddah Records where they thrived, thanks to a stable of songwriters and studio musicians. There they cranked out a string of woefully lyrical hits, which were dubbed "bubblegum." The Ohio Express became synonymous with this term, but the band was not much more than a touring representation of their recorded output. In fact, at various points in their career, the touring band didn't even know the material teenagers were expecting them to play during live performances.

Like the group they stole a record from, Kasenetz and Katz were a "rare breed." It seems fitting that this stolen record, inherited by the Ohio Express, was titled "**Beg, Borrow And Steal**."

BEG, BORROW AND STEAL

Open your smartphone camera & scan this QR code to listen to the song.

AN ANTI-DRUG PROTEST
Aired in February 2001

The 60s ran the gamut when it came to introducing new music trends, everything from the girl group phenomenon to dance crazes like the Twist, the Pony, and the Watusi, to the British Invasion and even the introspective Bob Dylan.

When the cause was right in their eyes, some recording artists seized the opportunity to make a statement in song. Many of these compositions were anti-establishment and aroused the concerns of those in the mainstream.

However, there was one "anti" recording made in 1967 that the mainstream welcomed with open arms. In fact, it is recognized as the first of its genre.

*****

In the mid-60s a very energetic and entertaining band emerged on the music scene. The band was from Portland, Oregon but soon found themselves in Los Angeles with their own TV show, *Where The Action Is.*

This band, which has often been referred to as America's answer to the British Invasion, was Paul Revere And The Raiders.

Between 1961 and 1973, they made it onto the Billboard Hot 100 twenty-four times, including five Top 10s and their #1 hit, "Indian Reservation" (1971).

Not unlike other artists of this decade, they too had a social conscience and seized their opportunity to make a statement in song against the use of drugs. This statement was one of their Top 10 hits and was embraced by the mainstream for it was pro-establishment even though it was "anti."

Confused? You won't be once you listen to Paul Revere And The Raiders sing "**Kicks**."

 KICKS

Open your smartphone camera & scan this QR code to listen to the song.

FROM THE WORLD OF FUNK

Aired in October 2007

One of the offshoots of rock music that surfaced in the early 70s was funk music, a blend of rock and R&B. It often partnered very soulful singers with bands that pushed the envelope in electronics.

In 1974 one group that burst onto the funk music scene featured a 21-year-old vocalist with a unique and what was to become an identifiable sound.

She continues to perform on her own but remains appreciative of that moment in time in 1974 when she and her group gained national recognition.

*****

Yvette Stevens was born on March 23, 1953 in the Chicago suburb of Great Lakes. She began performing professionally at fifteen and headed to Los Angeles in the early 70s, hooking up with a fledgling band of musicians. Two members of this group had previously been with the American Breed of "Bend Me, Shape Me" fame.

Over the years Stevens and her group would prove to be one of the most influential pop, rock, funk, and R&B groups, the central reasons being her amazing vocal talents and electrifying stage presence.

As a solo artist, Stevens has performed everything from bittersweet soul ballads, blistering pop covers, funk-drenched rap, and smoky jazz renderings to spiritual gospel, powerful Disco, syncopated funk, and steamy R&B.

In the summer of 1974, Stevens and her group found themselves on the Billboard Hot 100 at the #3 position with what has become one of the classic funk records of all time.

We know Yvette Stevens better by the name she adopted as a teen, Chaka Khan. At the age of 21, she fronted one of the great funk bands of all time, Rufus, to **"Tell Me Something Good."**

TELL ME SOME-THING GOOD

Open your smartphone camera & scan this QR code to listen to the song.

A GEM OF A RECORD

Aired in May 2001

In the early to mid-60s there was no producer hotter than Phil Spector. Famous for his "wall of sound," Spector produced some of the greatest acts and records that Rock & Roll has ever witnessed.

These performers included the Crystals ("He's A Rebel"), Bobby B. Soxx And The Blue Jeans ("Zip-A-Dee-Doo-Dah"), the Ronettes ("Be My Baby"), Darlene Love ("Today I Met The Boy I'm Gonna Marry"), and Curtis Lee ("Pretty Little Angel Eyes").

Spector eventually married Ronnie Bennett of the Ronettes and left producing in 1967. However, after a two-year hiatus, he was back in the studio. His deal with A&M records required him to produce some tunes with a singing group from Fort Wayne, Indiana.

*****

Spector started his musical career on the performer's side of the mike as part of a trio called the Teddy Bears who had a #1 smash hit in 1958 entitled "To Know Him Is To Love Him." For you trivia buffs, Sandy Nelson of "Teen Beat" fame plays the drums on this recording.

Spector soon became a well-known writer and producer. Upon his return to the studio in 1969, it didn't take him long to strike gold again.

Teamed with an incredibly talented group known as the Checkmates, Ltd., Spector's second record with them is considered to be one of his finest productions.

All the members of the group hailed from Fort Wayne, Indiana. However, after making their way to Las Vegas, they were discovered by singer Nancy Wilson who would go on to manage them for several years. She even secured them a recording contract with Capitol Records in 1966 but their releases failed to sell.

Then along came A&M and Spector, and the rest, as they say, was history. Their second release under Spector remained on the charts for over three months, peaking at the 13th position.

Unfortunately, all was not bliss, for the billing on the record label read "Sonny Charles & The Checkmates, Ltd.," which upset founding member and co-lead singer Bobby Stevens.

Even more upsetting is the fact that we don't hear this beautiful song enough. Listen to **"Black Pearl,"** and you'll see why it should be better known.

 BLACK PEARL

Open your smartphone camera & scan this QR code to listen to the song.

SURVIVAL OF THE HIPPEST

Aired in May 2018

In the fall of 1974, singer Shirley Goodman teamed up with a group of studio musicians and male vocalist, Jesus Alvarez, to give us Shirley (And Company), and the very popular 1975 Disco hit, "Shame, Shame, Shame."

This was the same Shirley Goodman who eighteen years earlier, in 1956, had teamed up with Leonard Lee and formed Shirley & Lee, finding success with "Let The Good Times Roll."

Jesus Alvarez soon left Shirley (And Company), changed his name to Jason Alvarez and became a pastor. He was replaced by Kenny Jeremiah.

*****

Like Goodman, Jeremiah was no stranger to success. A group he founded in the early 60s had a #4 hit on the Billboard charts in 1967.

Jeremiah's group was Philadelphia-based but started out playing in New York City in 1962 as the Dedications.

They changed their name in 1965 and began doing some recording, resulting in a million-seller that went #1 regionally in the New York/New Jersey area and #4 nationally.

The group eventually disbanded in the 70s but that did not stop Jeremiah, who joined Shirley (And Company). They continue to perform today.

Like the name of his successful group, you can say, without hesitation, that Jeremiah is one of the Soul Survivors and, like *Treasure Island Oldies,* continues to board the **"Expressway To Your Heart."**

 EXPRESSWAY TO YOUR HEART

Open your smartphone camera & scan this QR code to listen to the song.

GIRLS

WITH THE BIG

HITS

Although the early days of Rock & Roll appeared to be dominated by men on both sides of the microphone, there were a number of women who defied the odds and made names for themselves. White and black, some found success as solo artists and others in group settings.

The following ten segments span a number of music genres that ended up falling under the Rock & Roll umbrella – from R&B to pop to country.

LITTLE MISS DYNAMITE
Aired in July 2007

Professional sports like baseball, hockey, and basketball are filled with personalities who are often referred to by nicknames. In baseball, Mickey Mantle was often referred to as "The Mick," hockey's Wayne Gretzky was known as "The Great One," and basketball's legendary Wilt Chamberlain carried the moniker of "Wilt the Stilt" because of his height of more than seven feet.

The music industry also followed suit with Elvis Presley as "The King," Jerry Lee Lewis as "The Killer," and the late James Brown was revered as "The Godfather Of Soul."

Nicknames were given to female performers as well. One of the most notable was given to a young spunky gal who hit the Billboard pop charts at the age of thirteen in 1957 and has since become one of the predominant country crossover artists of our time.

*****

Female artists during the pop era of the late 40s and early 50s featured such singers as Joni James, Julie London, and Jo Stafford. One other artist from that period who displayed considerable energy when she performed was Teresa Brewer.

Subsequently, as a result of the acceptance of female vocalists and the introduction of Rock & Roll, a new wave of female singers came onto the scene.

One of them really took North America by storm in a style reminiscent of Teresa Brewer. By the time 1973 came along, she had made it on the Billboard Hot 100 fifty-five times and had two #1 hits to her credit.

Concurrently, she graced the country charts and was inducted into the Country Music Hall Of Fame. A staunch performer with a faithful following, she maintains her energy level and continues to live up to her nickname of the 60s ... "Little Miss Dynamite."

Her 1960 original release of "Rockin' Around The Christmas Tree" remains an institution during the festive season.

Sadly, this is not the case for one of her Top 10 hits of 1961. Rarely heard, it epitomizes her talent and upbeat nature. You will support this claim when you hear Brenda Lee, "Little Miss Dynamite," sing "**Dum Dum**."

 DUM DUM

Open your smartphone camera & scan this QR code to listen to the song.

ONE OF THE FIRST FEMALE R&B VOCAL GROUPS

Aired in September 2005

It's pretty common knowledge that many of the great Doo Wop groups of the late 50s got their "sound" by hanging out on street corners or subway platforms in New York and other major U.S. cities, singing four-part harmonies without any instruments.

Unlike their male counterparts, girls weren't able to "hang out" on street corners at all hours, practicing. For one prominent female group, school locker rooms and gymnasiums were the venues of choice for honing their skills. Not only did they practice, they wrote and subsequently released their own material in the late 50s.

*****

Arlene Smith (lead), Lois Harris, Sonia Goring, Jackie Landry, and Rene Minus began their musical journey in their preteens while attending choir practice at St. Anthony of Padua School in Bronx, New York.

By 1957, they had been singing together for more than seven years. While in high school, much of their practice took place in the girls' locker room. Arlene Smith was also a member of the girls' basketball team and, win or lose, the group would sing after every game.

The strength of the group, apart from its vocal presence, was the writing ability of lead singer Smith. There weren't many girl groups in the mid-50s and even fewer that wrote their own material. Smith contributed both words and music, and the combination of her classical and gospel background with simple yet poignant lyrics made her more successful at sixteen than she could have possibly imagined.

The group's breakout record on the Billboard pop charts occurred in September of 1957 with the release of "He's Gone." However, it was in January of the next year that their smash hit, "Maybe," graced the airwaves.

Penned by Smith, this record became their signature song and launched the group nationally. It also was the first song by a girl group to sell a million records.

In addition to this, *Rolling Stone* magazine once described Arlene Smith as the best female vocalist in the history of Rock & Roll, dubbing her the "Queen of Doo Wop."

You may not remember Arlene Smith by name but you might remember her group, the Chantels, and their classic 1958 million seller, "**Maybe**."

 MAYBE

Open your smartphone camera & scan this QR code to listen to the song.

LOVE FOR A SONG

Aired in March 2020

This moment in time features a record that made it to #1 on the Billboard Hot 100 in November of 1962. How it got there and who got it there is quite a story.

*****

Early in 1962, Gene Pitney wrote a song for the Shirelles. However, the girls turned down the opportunity to record it. Phil Spector, an old friend of Pitney's, had heard the demo and believed the song would be a hit.

Finding out that the song was now being earmarked by Liberty Records for up-and-coming singer Vicki Carr, the race was on for Spector to get his version released as soon as possible.

With two Top 20 hits already under his belt with a new East Coast girl group, Spector set the wheels in motion to produce the song in Los Angeles. You can just imagine how shocked he was when his East Coast girls balked at coming to Los Angeles because of a fear of flying. But that did not stop Spector. He got the premiere female backup singing group in Los Angeles, a trio at the time, to provide the vocals.

His trio of artists - Darlene Wright, Fanita James, and Gracia Nitzche - were known as the Blossoms, a group that had a few personnel changes over the years. During the 50s and 60s, they made a career out of singing backup for many artists from Paul Anka to Elvis Presley. Their versatility enabled them to be a choral group one minute for Ed Townsend on "For Your Love" and to produce a surf sound for many of Jan & Dean's hits. However, it was this Phil Spector production in the summer of 1962 that made them the ultimate uncredited group of the 60s.

You see, when the song was released, it erroneously came out as being sung by the Crystals, who were most surprised. In fact, it caused a challenge for the East Coast group because lead singer, Barbara Alston, could not match the singing voice of Darlene Wright of the Blossoms on the record. It also propelled fifteen-year-old Dolores "LaLa" Brooks of the Crystals to take the lead on the song when the group toured.

Darlene Wright, motivated by Phil Spector, changed her name and went on to become Darlene Love.

Looking back on this story, you can readily see that the title of the #1 record aptly describes Phil Spector because **"He's A Rebel."**

 HE'S A REBEL

Open your smartphone camera & scan this QR code to listen to the song.

THE FIRST RAP SONG?

Aired in March 2002

One of North American broadcasting's all-time favorite personalities was Art Linkletter. His long-running *House Party* show was a daytime standby and graced both radio and television from 1945 until 1970. His ability to get members of the studio audience to perform mad stunts for prizes was unparalleled. However, he is probably best remembered for those precious interviews with children.

In 1954, on the TV version of his show, Art introduced America to eight-year-old Geraldine Ann Pasquale. Five years later she had a Top 10 hit at the age of thirteen.

*****

Geraldine Ann Pasquale was born in Chicago on February 17, 1946. Her family moved to California when she was three. At the age of eight, under the name Geri Pace, she got to sing her first Gold Star Records release – "Merry-Go-Round Go Round" – on Art Linkletter's *House Party* TV show.

As the 50s progressed, Pace discovered Rock & Roll and R&B, hoping that one day she could record something with "guts" along the lines of Wanda Jackson's "Let's Have A Party" or Brenda Lee's "Dynamite."

What was to be Pace's fifteen minutes of fame was a 1959 tune that was exactly opposite to her desires and one that she did not think too much of. She also wasn't thrilled with her new name. In her words, "I thought the song was dumb. I didn't like the song. And I didn't like [my] name ... I look back on it now and it was really the first rap song. I talked all the verses and only sang the chorus."

It proved to be the right thing at the right time for it stayed 19 weeks on the charts, peaking at the #3 position.

Geraldine Ann Pasquale is better known to most of us as Dodie Stevens. It's hard to believe that we have Art Linkletter to thank for discovering our first rap recording artist with the "talking" hit "**Pink Shoe Laces.**"

 PINK SHOE LACES

Open your smartphone camera & scan this QR code to listen to the song.

CHANGING TIMES

Aired in May 2005

Many times, the cover versions by white artists in the early days of Rock & Roll became more nationally recognized and commercially successful than the original releases by black artists.

It was a different time back then ... but times were a-changin' ... and those times changed for one black female artist in particular.

*****

In the mid-50s, music recordings by black artists were often referred to as "race records," given that they contained lyrics that were considered, back then, to be somewhat risqué.

In the early 50s, bandleader and talent scout, Johnny Otis (of "Willie & The Hand Jive" fame) discovered a Los Angeles-born teenager who could really belt out R&B. In 1954 she released a record originally entitled "Roll With Me Henry." It was subsequently retitled as "The Wallflower" and then again as "Dance With Me Henry." Although this teenager ended up with a single that topped the R&B charts, her original version was no match for the nationally and commercially successful cover of "Dance With Me Henry" by white artist Georgia Gibbs in 1955.

Initially you might think "how sad," but times were changing and thanks to the likes of Georgia Gibbs and

Pat Boone, black music and black artists were getting recognized.

In tandem with the discovery and national acceptance of black music in America in the 60s, this Los Angeles-born teenager had a run of 28 nationally charted records that ranked her third, just behind Aretha Franklin and Dionne Warwick, as the most prolific female R&B vocalist of her era. Her name was Etta James.

Her most successful song from that decade was a tune written by Clarence Carter and released in 1967. It stayed on the charts for 14 weeks and was featured in the opening of the Jane Fonda/Jennifer Lopez 2005 movie, *Monster-in-Law*. It's titled "**Tell Mama**."

 TELL MAMA

Open your smartphone camera & scan this QR code to listen to the song.

NORTHERN SOUL
Aired in November 2014

In 1977 tragedy hit the music industry when Marc Bolan, lead vocalist/guitarist of the glam rock band, T. Rex, died in a car crash in England. T. Rex's big 1972 hit had been "Bang A Gong (Get It On)."

The driver of that car on that ill-fated night was his girl-friend, Gloria Jones, an American singer/songwriter/pianist from Los Angeles who played with the band from time to time.

In 1964 while in her late teens, this songstress released a record in the U.S. for Uptown Records, a subsidiary of Capitol/EMI. The record went nowhere in North America. However, many years later during the Northern Soul movement in England, it was rebirthed.

*****

Northern Soul is a music and dance movement that emerged from the British Mod scene, initially in Northern England in the late 1960s. Northern Soul mainly consists of a particular style of black American soul music based on the heavy beat and fast tempo of the mid-1960s Motown Sound.

The term "Northern Soul" originated from the record shop known as Soul City in Covent Garden, London, which was run by journalist Dave Godin. In a 2002 interview, Godin said he had first come up with the term

"Northern Soul" in 1968, to help employees at Soul City differentiate the more modern, funkier sounds from the smoother, Motown-influenced soul of a few years earlier.

Recently, a movie titled *Northern Soul* was released in England and has become a hit. Also, BBC4 released a documentary on Northern Soul.

Gloria Jones is featured in this British documentary. It is said that her following was so strong that she was proclaimed the "Queen Of Northern Soul."

And that 1964 record that went nowhere in North America was the driving force that propelled Marc Almond to re-release the record with his partner, David Ball, after hearing it in a nightclub in Northern England.

Their version went on to #1 status worldwide in 1982. It was officially #8 on the Billboard Hot 100 and remained on those charts for 43 weeks.

We know Marc Almond and David Ball better as the group Soft Cell. That song, originally recorded by Gloria Jones in 1964, was **"Tainted Love."**

 TAINTED LOVE

Open your smartphone camera & scan this QR code to listen to the song.

THE LAST #1 RECORD ON A 78

Aired in February 2002

By 1950, following Columbia Broadcasting's lead, almost all record companies had gone over to 33 1/3 recordings. To further confuse the public as to what type of recording and what kind of record player to buy, RCA introduced the 45 in the middle of 1949.

Despite the confusion, there was one thing that appeared certain: the 78 was on its way out.

With newer jukeboxes being made for the 45 market and older ones being reconfigured for these new seven-inch discs, the 50s would be the last decade for production of 78s in North America.

The last record to be issued on a 78 that reached #1 status was recorded in 1956.

*****

Columbia Broadcasting began its search for a practical, slow-speed microgroove recording in 1944. Their objective was to produce a record that would play classical compositions for up to half an hour without having to turn the record over. They achieved their goal and introduced what became known as the LP (Long Play) in 1948.

Moreover, it had other advantages over the 78 – it was made out of a light, unbreakable plastic and the tone arm required less weight, thanks to the microgrooves, thus improving the quality of the sound.

Having no intention of letting Columbia steal the show, RCA came out with its own version of the microgroove, smaller at seven inches in diameter and a little faster at 45 rpm. People still say that RCA did the industry an injustice by forcing a new recording format on consumers.

Throughout it all, RCA maintained that the 45 was more suitable for popular recordings and could co-exist peacefully with the 33 1/3 rpm LP, which was, after all, for more serious music.

During the transition period of the early 50s, these technological changes put many record publishers in a quandary as to what format they should use to release their new songs. They realized that they could put a number of songs on an LP, so it came down to deciding whether to release a single version of a particular song on a 45 or on a 78. In most cases, they released them on both until the 78 officially went the way of the dodo bird and the 45 captured the market.

The last #1 record to be issued on a 78, as well as on a 45, was released in 1956. Fittingly, it was a pop tune that crossed over and was accepted by the new Rock & Roll generation – a generation that was obsessed with a new kid on the block by the name of Elvis Presley.

That #1 record was Gogi Grant's **"The Wayward Wind."**

 THE WAYWARD WIND

Open your smartphone camera & scan this QR code to listen to the song.

THE YOUNGEST AT #1

Aired in May 2003

Did You know that 50 years ago in 1953, Patti Page's "How Much Is That Doggie In The Window" topped the charts? In fact it was #1 for 8 straight weeks.

Or how about the #1 tune from thirty years ago? It was #1 for 4 weeks. The group was Dawn featuring Tony Orlando and the song that seemed to be played at every wedding during the 70s was "Tie A Yellow Ribbon Round The Ole Oak Tree."

However, it is the story about the #1 song from forty years ago (1963) that is the real attention getter. Its rise to the top of the charts certified the artist as the youngest female singer ever to have a #1 single on the Billboard pop charts. She was fifteen years, one month, and thirteen days old.

*****

Margaret Battavio grew up in Lansdale, Pennsylvania. In late April of 1963, at the age of 15, she had a #1 nationwide hit, the timing of which allowed her to edge out Brenda Lee as the youngest female singer with a #1 single to her credit.

Her sudden rise to stardom was a result of her being heard singing at a friend's wedding and her dad being persuaded to allow her to audition for RCA.

Her first song went nowhere but soon another song wound up on the desk of Hugo and Luigi's at RCA. The song was already a big hit in France for Petula Clark, who recorded it under the name of "Chariot." English lyrics were added and the song was released by Margaret Battavio on January 22, 1963 – it was #1 by the end of April.

At the age of twenty Battavio married her manager, Arnie Harris, and they moved to Germany, staying there for twelve years. At a song festival in 1971, a man from France introduced himself to her and thanked her for her #1 hit of 1963. Puzzled, she asked the man why he was thanking her. The man, Paul Mauriat (from "Love Is Blue" fame) revealed to her for the first time that he had written the song as an instrumental under the nom de plume, Del Roma.

Yes, Paul Mauriat received #1 status in America as a songwriter thanks to Margaret Battavio, whose stage name, which she legally adopted, was taken from her month of birth. That's why she is better known as Little Peggy March. And she will always be remembered for her smash hit from forty years ago, "**I Will Follow Him.**"

 I WILL FOLLOW HIM

Open your smartphone camera & scan this QR code to listen to the song.

ONE OF JOHN LENNON'S FAVORITES

Aired in May 2006

The name Rosalie Hamlin is not a name that many would recognize in the music field. However, thanks to her tenacity and talent, she was able to transform a poem that she wrote into one of the classic teenage ballads of all time, a ballad that was later re-recorded by John Lennon, who stated that this singer was one of his favorite American artists.

*****

Rosalie Hamlin was born on July 21, 1945 in Oregon and spent her early childhood growing up in Alaska. She moved to the San Diego area with her family in the late 50s.

Early in 1960 at the age of fourteen, her mother gave her an old upright piano and she began taking instruction from her aunt. However, she had already acquired a taste for performing by singing lead for a group of musicians at local clubs in and around the San Diego area.

Inspired by their community acceptance, Hamlin and the group decided to record a poem that she had written about a teenage love. The recording took place in San Marcos, California in an old airplane hangar that had been converted into a studio. The final version of the recording was generated from an old two-track machine and took over thirty takes to master.

With recording in hand but no record deal, the group

took one of their 45s to the local Kresge store in San Diego and convinced the store manager to let his teenage customers listen to the song in one of their listening booths. As fate would have it, a distributor for Highland Records was in the store at the time and happened to hear the song.

Young and naïve, the group gave their master to Highland representatives without signing a contract. Three weeks later they heard the legendary Alan Freed promoting the record on air. Subsequently, they managed to sit down with Highland Records executives and sign a deal. Hamlin had to have her mother sign for her because she was not yet sixteen.

What was disturbing about the signing was that she was only recognized as the performer and not listed as the writer. This took years to straighten out before she was able to receive the royalties that she deserved. In addition to this, the group disbanded before the record was ever released.

Rosalie Hamlin is better known in music circles simply as "Rosie" - her group that she was with in the summer of 1960 was called the Originals.

Hamlin's favorite remake of her song was by John Lennon, a version that was produced by Phil Spector in the 70s and released posthumously in 1986. On the *Menlove Ave.* album, Lennon's voice can be heard saying: "This is one of my all-time favorite songs ... my love to Rosie wherever she may be." You could say that Rosie was John Lennon's **"Angel Baby."**

 ANGEL BABY

Open your smartphone camera & scan this QR code to listen to the song.

THE MOST SUCCESSFUL CROSSOVER HIT

Aired in May 2001

In these segments we have featured or made reference to a number of crossover tunes, that is, records that were successful on more than one of the Billboard charts.

For the most part two charts were usually involved, such as The Hot 100 and the Billboard country charts or the Hot 100 and the R&B charts or one of the Adult Contemporary charts.

Some classic examples of artists who enjoyed this type of crossover success were Johnny Cash and Jerry Lee Lewis (country crossovers), Ray Charles (R&B crossovers), and Bobby Darin and Petula Clark (Adult Contemporary crossovers).

However, the most successful crossover hit on Billboard's four major charts came from a country singer in the early 60s.

*****

In January of 1963, a 31-year-old country singer introduced a song to the nation that lasted 17 weeks on the Billboard Hot 100 and climbed to the #2 position during that period. That same song also hit the #2 position on the Billboard country charts.

However, what is most amazing is that this song simultaneously reached the #4 position on the R&B charts and the sacred #1 position on the Adult Contemporary charts, thus making it the most successful crossover tune of all time.

The artist was no slouch in the country music circles, either. In fact, she charted 41 times on the country charts from 1958 through 1976.

Her 1963 smash hit even had an impact in England, with Herman's Hermits doing a cover version of the song on their 1964 debut album.

The artist was none other than Skeeter Davis, whose 1963 claim to fame is the tear-jerking ballad "**The End Of The World.**"

THE END OF
THE WORLD

Open your smartphone camera & scan this QR code to listen to the song.

COUNTRY

CROSSOVERS

Teenagers were the driving force behind Rock & Roll but their tastes were far from narrow. Numerous country records and country stars made their way to the Billboard Hot 100 thanks to the teenager who liked the sound of the music. This was significant for country musicians because record sales went up exponentially if they were able to get a song to cross over to the Rock & Roll charts.

In the segments in this chapter, we feature ten great country artists who not only had their songs cross over to the Hot 100, but also ended up with at least one Top 10 hit on both the country and pop charts.

TRAVELIN' & TRUCKIN'

Aired in June 2002

Back in the 50s and early 60s the term "crossover records" was popularized to describe songs that appealed to fans of different types of music. In the case of country music, there were a number of significant songs that made their way on to the Billboard pop charts during that period.

One particular type of country music was the truck drivin' song. Accomplished country performers such as Red Sovine with "Giddy-Up Go," Dave Dudley with "Six Days On The Road," and the legendary Hank Snow with his classic "I've Been Everywhere" found their way to mainstream charts.

But it wasn't always the recognized country artists that got the airplay for songs of mass appeal. Such was the case for a country session musician who made the Top 10 with his classic truckin' song that was introduced to the nation in late 1958.

*****

During the 50s country singers and frequent *Grand Ole Opry* performers like Grandpa Jones, T. Texas Tyler, Clyde Moody, and honky-tonker Hawkshaw Hawkins were much in demand. What these artists had in common was an extremely capable and trusted sideman.

The talents of this backup musician and session performer were also recognized by Jimmy Dean (of "Big Bad

John" fame). In 1955 he became a regular on Jimmy Dean's daily TV show out of Washington, DC. Two years later the show went national and the performer was offered a contract with Monument Records.

It was that contract that allowed this musician to "cross over" with his debut recording that was released in late 1958. The recording was yet another travelin'/truck drivin' song. It went to #5 on the country charts and soared to #4 on the pop charts, staying there for 20 weeks. Ironically, the song was based on a 19th century tune that originated in the British Isles.

Throughout the 60s this artist remained one the busiest accompanists and session guitarists in Nashville. For you trivia buffs, he is also the originator and manufacturer of a flat top guitar named after him.

That session guitarist was Billy Grammer and in November of 1958 he had a huge crossover country hit with "**Gotta Travel On.**"

 GOTTA TRAVEL ON

Open your smartphone camera & scan this QR code to listen to the song.

ELVIS IN DISGUISE?
Aired in July 2012

In June of 1993 we lost one of the greatest country music singers of all time from an abdominal aneurysm at the age of 59.

Prior to switching over to country music in 1965, this artist had been a very successful pop singer from 1957 through 1962, making it onto the Billboard Hot 100 charts 14 times including two Top 10 hits and a #1 hit in 1958. As a country singer he had forty #1 hits, a record that was finally broken by George Strait in 2006.

In his early days, this legendary performer recorded at Sun Studios around the same time as Carl Perkins, Elvis Presley, Jerry Lee Lewis, and Johnny Cash. He eventually developed a sound that led him to a record deal with MGM Records.

For a brief period, some thought he was Elvis Presley recording under a different name. A late release in 1959 certainly supported that claim.

*****

Born Harold Lloyd Jenkins in 1933, our pop-turned-country icon had two passions – music and baseball. After finishing high school he was offered a contract to play baseball for the Philadelphia Phillies. However, fate stepped in and he was drafted into the army. He never went back to baseball but proceeded to focus all his attention on honing his musical skills.

Upon signing with MGM in 1957 he decided on a name change. Allegedly he picked his name from two cities on the map – Conway, Arkansas and Twitty, Texas. That's how Conway Twitty was "born."

His second release to make it onto the Billboard charts went to #1 in 1958. "It's Only Make Believe" was written by Twitty and his drummer Jack Nance, between sets during a gig in Hamilton, Ontario, Canada. The song stayed on the charts for 21 straight weeks and started the rumor mill about Elvis recording under another name.

To add fuel to the fire, the following year, in 1959, Twitty released a song that was originally recorded by Elvis for the movie *King Creole*. Elvis' version, although never released, was titled "Danny."

Conway Twitty's release went to #6 on the Billboard Hot 100. It continues to be mistaken as an Elvis song despite being retitled "**Lonely Blue Boy**."

 LONELY BLUE BOY

Open your smartphone camera & scan this QR code to listen to the song.

A HURTIN' RECORD

Aired in October 2002

In the 40s, 50s, and 60s there were many country songs that crossed over to the pop charts. Some of these successful crossovers fell into the country category known as "hurtin' records" – you know, those songs where boy loses his girl, all of his money, and his horse to boot.

One prolific writer of these tunes charted no less than 82 times on the country charts from 1956 through 1976. Fourteen of these tunes crossed over to the pop charts.

Of those fourteen that charted, there was only one that he did not write.

*****

In 1956 at the age of 26, a young singer/songwriter/guitarist from Shelby, North Carolina had a Top 10 country hit. He reissued this sentimental record in 1960 and scored again. Three years later, Patsy Cline recorded it as well. The song? "Sweet Dreams."

But that was just the beginning. He went on to write and record other tearjerkers such as "I Can't Stop Loving You" (which also became a big hit for Ray Charles), "Oh, Lonesome Me," "Blue Blue Day," and "Lonesome Number One."

His "hurtin' records" that crossed over to the pop charts, were all produced by the legendary Chet Atkins.

The only record that he had on the pop charts that he did not write came out in 1961. If you're lucky, you will hear it on some of the better country and oldie stations. It was written by Hal David and Paul Hampton for the legendary Don Gibson who took charge in arranging the song and guiding you through the **"Sea Of Heartbreak."**

 SEA OF HEART-
BREAK

Open your smartphone camera & scan this QR code to listen to the song.

FROM ROCKABILLY TO BALLADS
Aired in April 2014

This moment in time features an American country singer who was equally adept at singing ballads, honky-tonk songs, and Rockabilly pop tunes.

After recording under the name of Terry Preston in the early 50s, he began working with the likes of Tennessee Ernie Ford. In 1957 he hit pay dirt with a song that crossed over from the country charts to the pop charts.

*****

This country crossover artist spent five years in the U.S. Merchant Marines during World War II, entertaining troops on transport ships. That's where he created and played an outspoken comic hayseed by the name of Simon Crum.

He subsequently developed this character during his days as a deejay in Missouri and then in Bakersfield, California.

In the early 50s he released some humorous records under the Simon Crum name. In addition to this, he made TV appearances as this character on a number of country music shows – some of which you can catch on YouTube.

In 1953, he also began recording under his given name. It is under this name that we know him best. He made it onto the country charts 49 times over the 22-year period from 1953–1975, and he crossed over to the pop charts on four different occasions.

By far his biggest success was his first crossover record in 1957. It remained on both the country and pop charts for 27 weeks. It went to #1 on the country charts and peaked at the 4th position on the Billboard Hot 100.

This record is recognized as one of the classic hurtin' ballads left behind by the late great Ferlin Husky who is now "**Gone.**"

 GONE

Open your smartphone camera & scan this QR code to listen to the song.

MR. SMOOTH
Aired in May 2019

One of the fascinations in Rock & Roll is the regional success of certain songs - how a song could be in the Top 10 in one market, while barely making a splash in another.

One of the more unusual circumstances in this regard relates to a song by one of America's great country-pop singer/songwriters of the 50s, 60s, and 70s.

*****

Born in Guilford, Missouri in 1928 and raised in Glendale, Arizona, he began singing and playing the guitar at the age of fourteen. It wasn't until 1972, at the age of 44, he had his one and only #1 country hit, "If You Leave Me Tonight I'll Cry," a song featured in "The Tune In Dan's Café," an episode from the series *Night Gallery*. It was also his last record to chart on the Billboard Hot 100, crossing over and peaking at the 38th position.

Often referred to as Mr. Smooth, he graced the pop charts early in his career with such classics as "How The Time Flies" (1958), "Primrose Lane" (1959), and "In The Misty Moonlight" (1964). The artist, of course, is the late, great Jerry Wallace.

In 1965, he made his debut on the country charts and remained there for the next 15 years, charting 35 times during that period.

Ironically, one of his country-sounding releases that made the Billboard Hot 100 in December of 1962 did not make the country charts. Co-written by country movie star Audie Murphy, it could best be described as a "hurtin' record." What's more ironic is that it was Wallace's fourth-most successful song on the Billboard pop charts in the U.S. However, in Toronto, Canada, it was his most successful recording, outperforming all of his charted hits.

Back in 1962, Mr. Smooth, Jerry Wallace, was at his peak, dusting off those **"Shutters And Boards."**

 SHUTTERS AND BOARDS

Open your smartphone camera & scan this QR code to listen to the song.

THE VELVET VOICE

Aired in July 2010

If there is one color that has had a tremendous impact on music and its different genres, it has to be the color blue. Along the instrumental lines, we were blessed with the "Blue Tango" (a remake hit for Bill Black's Combo in 1960); jazz gave us "Blue Moon" which also was a hit in the categories of pop and Doo Wop thanks to the Marcels; and, of course, there was the Rock & Roll classic, "Blue Suede Shoes," an original hit for Carl Perkins and successfully covered by Elvis Presley and others.

When it comes to country music and its "hurtin' records," blue is by far the dominant color. It was an alternative definition of blue, one of "being down and out," that proved to be the path to gold for many country artists.

***** *

Despite dying tragically in a plane crash in Nashville on July 31, 1964 at the age of 39, a country artist was able to make it onto the country charts 80 times, including ten #1 hits.

Twenty-three of his country hits (including eight of his #1s) crossed over to the pop charts – all were produced by Chet Atkins.

Our artist went "blue" in 1958 with a record that went to #2 on the country charts and became his third crossover hit on the pop charts. The song featured his warm, velvety voice, a voice that could bring a tear to your eye.

That country artist was the legendary Gentleman Jim Reeves. For many of us, Jim Reeves is a lost treasure and there will always be a place in our hearts for this **"Blue Boy."**

BLUE BOY

Open your smartphone camera & scan this QR code to listen to the song.

FIRE OF CONTROVERSY
Aired in September 2017

This segment features a recording artist who was a singer/songwriter, an actor, and an author. Recognized for influencing American music in the 20th century, he holds the rare distinction of being inducted into the Country Music Hall Of Fame, the Rock & Roll Hall Of Fame, and the Gospel Hall Of Fame.

Twelve of his fourteen #1 country singles crossed over to the Billboard pop charts. Included in that dynamic dozen was a 1963 song that has a background steeped in controversy.

* * * * *

That 1963 song was first recorded by Anita Carter, June Carter Cash's sister. When the song appeared to be going nowhere, our featured artist, Johnny Cash, decided to release his own version.

Cash's version shot up the country charts and remained at the #1 position for 7 straight weeks. It soon crossed over the pop charts and went Top 20.

The writing of the song is credited to June Carter Cash and Merle Kilgore. June Carter Cash, who was falling in love with Johnny at the time, tells quite a story of how she was inspired to co-write this song of passion.

However, Johnny Cash's first wife, Vivian Liberto, in her book *I Walked The Line* states, "To this day, it confounds me to hear the elaborate details June told of writing that song for Johnny. She didn't write that song any more than I did. The truth is, Johnny wrote that song while pilled-up and drunk, about a certain private female body part. All those years of her claiming she wrote it herself, and she probably never knew what the song was really about." Liberto also claims that Cash decided to give June co-writer status because she needed the money.

Not to be outdone, co-writer Merle Kilgore has often stirred the pot about this song during live performances by mock dedicating it to the makers of Preparation H.

One thing that we do know for sure was that this song was a hit and Johnny Cash will definitely be remembered for the "**Ring Of Fire.**"

 RING OF FIRE

Open your smartphone camera & scan this QR code to listen to the song.

THE STORYTELLER
Aired in March 2003

Spring is a glorious time of the year - but not in all parts of North America, as Johnny Horton pointed out in one of his classic 1959 ballads.

*****

Johnny Horton is a true Rockabilly legend. He crossed the line of radio formats in the late 50s and early 60s with his story-telling songs. Much of his up-tempo material did not appeal to the traditionalists but somebody once wrote that "he was ten years older than most of the rockabillies but with his cowboy hat hiding a receding hairline, he more or less looked the part."

We lost Horton at the age of 35 on November 11, 1960 in an automobile accident. Sadly, this tragedy made his wife, Billie Jean Horton (nee Jones), a widow of a country star for a second time as she had been previously married to another country legend, Hank Williams Sr., who was found dead on January 1, 1953 in a car he had commissioned to get him to a New Year's Day performance.

Horton's "saga" songs have certainly guaranteed that he will not be forgotten. Most of us readily remember him for his 1960 release of "North To Alaska," the title song of the classic John Wayne film. The song went to #4 on the Billboard pop charts that year. It also topped the U.S. country charts for five weeks.

Horton had crossed over to the pop charts a year earlier, in April of 1959, with a #1 smash hit, "The Battle Of New Orleans."

But that wasn't his first #1 hit. He had achieved that status three months earlier on the country charts with a haunting, chilly reminder of what spring is like in other parts of North America.

In this song, the incomparable Johnny Horton makes it quite clear that "**When It's Springtime In Alaska (It's Forty Below).**"

Epilogue: If you listen closely, the last line of the song may seem to foreshadow Johnny Horton's passing. By the time March had rolled around in 1961, it was "springtime in Alaska and [he was] six feet below."

WHEN IT'S SPRING-TIME IN ALASKA (IT'S FORTY BELOW)

Open your smartphone camera & scan this QR code to listen to the song.

LIFE SUMMED UP IN SONG
Aired in April 2006

One of the essential ingredients for artistic success in music, aside from talent, has been the establishing of a strong relationship with the songwriting community.

During the late 50s and throughout the 60s, this community was blessed with the likes of Phil Spector, Gerry Goffin, Carole King, and Leiber & Stoller who shaped the path that music would take during this era.

However, like the performers they wrote for, composers and lyricists had to start somewhere too – and their beginnings are just as fascinating.

*****

While working at the famous Paramount Music Company in 1957, a twenty-nine-year-old composer teamed up with an accomplished lyricist. It was the beginning of a partnership that would span four decades highlighted by the collaboration on twenty Top 40 Billboard hits over a ten-year period for Dionne Warwick.

Of course, we speak of the dynamic duo, composer Burt Bacharach and lyricist Hal David.

Although mostly associated with the pop and contemporary music scene of the late 50s, 60s, and 70s, Burt Bacharach and Hal David's first recognized triumph was actually a country record that crossed over to the pop charts in 1957.

The song was #1 on the country charts for 4 weeks and peaked at #15 on the Billboard pop charts. What is more impressive is the fact that this recording remained on both the country and pop charts for 23 and 24 straight weeks respectively.

Thanks to Marty Robbins, both Bacharach and David could probably say that it was just the beginning of "**The Story Of My Life.**"

Open your smartphone camera & scan this QR code to listen to the song.

CARDS TALK

Aired in September 2007

Gale Storm and Bonnie Guitar both had Top 10 successes recording "Dark Moon," which peaked at the #4 and #6 positions respectively in 1957 on the Billboard pop charts. A ballad, it was written by a songwriting pipefitter who was born in Rains, Utah and raised in Salt Lake City.

That same year, 1957, the songwriter recorded one of his own tunes for Dot Records. Unfortunately, it bombed and he went back to songwriting and pipefitting. Unbeknownst to the artist, his original recording was also destined to be Top 10, but not until February of 1963.

*****

Our featured artist's name is Ned Miller. His mother taught him the guitar, and by his teenage years he was writing songs. After serving three years in the Marines, Miller studied for two years and became a pipefitter.

After his tune "Dark Moon" hit the Top 10, Miller decided to release another original recording of his own. It sold poorly and many wrote the record off.

In late 1962 Fabor Robison was persuaded by Miller to re-release the record on his own private Fabor label. To the amazement of all parties involved, the record took off, reaching #2 on the country charts and #6 on the Billboard pop charts. It was a huge hit in Canada and held down the

#1 position for 3 weeks in Toronto. It made it to #2 in the UK where it was ranked as the sixth-most-played song of 1963.

Given this six-year delay, many would have bet that success was not in the cards for Ned Miller, but thanks to that re-release he went **"From A Jack To A King."**

Open your smartphone camera & scan this QR code to listen to the song.

FROM ACROSS
THE P●ND

The Rock & Roll phenomenon and evolution was not confined to North America. It soon became international, with the term "Rock & Roll" requiring no translation wherever you travelled.

By the early 60s, "Teenage America" became exposed to songs from international locations, initially from the UK and led by the Beatles.

Beatlemania proved to be a significant period in Rock & Roll history and the catalyst for what was to be called the British Invasion. At the time, if you came from England, played Rock & Roll music, and talked with an accent, you were "in" with the North American public.

This phenomenon put a lot of pressure on North American artists and groups to be successful and make it on the charts. The following ten moments in time illustrate the wide range of overseas talent that found an audience in North America.

A NAME GIRLS LIKE
Aired in March 2013

Celebrating St. Patrick's Day would not be complete without featuring one of the most successful Irish trios that hailed from Dublin.

In 1957 brothers Con and Dec Cluskey joined forces with countryman John Stokes and formed the Harmonichords, a classical-styled instrumental harmonica act.

While still in their teens they appeared on *The Ed Sullivan St. Patrick's Day* special that was filmed in Dublin and broadcast on March 15, 1959 in North America. On that night they did a rendition of "Danny Boy."

Five years later they were on the Billboard Hot 100 with the first of nine releases.

*****

In the early 60s the trio from Dublin abandoned their harmonicas, changed their name and started putting out a series of successful songs that made it onto the music charts in Europe, Australia, South America, South Africa, and parts of the USSR, as well as in Canada and the United States.

Their debut on Billboard on April 18, 1964 went to #10 and stayed on the charts for 13 weeks. Their song "Diane" was a remake of a 1928 #2 hit by the Nat Shilkret Orchestra.

A year later, in 1965, they again reached back into the vault and took a 1928 song written by Irving Berlin that went to #1 for Tommy Dorsey in 1937 and #2 on the R&B charts (#13 on the pop charts) for the Four Tunes in 1953. The title of this song was "Marie."

Maybe changing their name in 1962 to the Bachelors at the suggestion of Dick Rowe, then the A&R man at Decca Records, was what the doctor ordered because in Dick Rowe's words, "that's the kind of boy girls like."

And the girls sure liked the Bachelors' records, especially those girls named "Diane" and "**Marie**."

 MARIE

Open your smartphone camera & scan this QR code to listen to the song.

THE BIGGEST FEMALE UK HIT OF THE 60S

Aired in May 2019

This moment in time features one of Burt Bacharach and Hal David's greatest recordings, a recording that had worldwide success – a success that was divided between two artists.

*****

The original version was recorded by Dionne Warwick in the U.S. in 1963 and went Top 10 in January of the following year – Warwick's first record to go Top 10.

Meanwhile, in England, an up-and-coming singer from Liverpool reached #1 status on the UK charts with her version of the Bacharach/David song in February of 1964, making it onto those charts a week before Dionne Warwick's version was released in England.

As the story goes, being bested in Britain has been a permanent sore point for Warwick. And, it is ironic that Bacharach, himself an American, backed the English artist on this British release.

Warwick lamented that the English version was so close to her original recording that if she had coughed or a wrong instrumental note had been played, it would have found its way into the remake.

A scout for record producer George Martin initially suggested that the song would be a perfect vehicle for

Shirley Bassey. However, Martin thought otherwise, deeming the composition to be a perfect debut record for his budding Liverpool singer.

The singer was born Priscilla Maria Veronica White – quite a mouthful and probably why she is better known by her stage name, Cilla Black.

In May of 2010, research published by BBC Radio 2 revealed that the biggest female UK chart hit of the 60s was Cilla Black's version of "**Anyone Who Had A Heart.**"

ANYONE WHO HAD A HEART

Open your smartphone camera & scan this QR code to listen to the song.

BABY COME BACK

Aired in April 2010

After moving to Barbados in 1982, singer/songwriter Eddy Grant went on to have a monster Billboard pop hit in 1983 with "Electric Avenue."

Although it didn't make it to #1, it held the #2 position on both the UK and U.S. charts. It remained on the Billboard Hot 100 for 22 weeks.

However, this was not the first time Grant had been recognized nationally in North America and in the UK. The first time this occurred was fifteen years earlier in 1968 with a song that he wrote.

*****

Eddy Grant was born in Plaisance, Guyana and moved to London, England in 1960. In 1967 he formed his own group, an interracial British-Jamaican rock quintet. It was this group that gained national airplay in both the UK and North America.

Although he was a teetotaler and a vegetarian, Grant had some health problems in the early 70s and was forced to slow down and re-evaluate his lifestyle. A shrewd businessman, Grant went on to form his own record label, Ice Records, and build the Blue Wave Studio Complex when he moved to Barbados in the early 80s. Over the years he has produced for Sting, Mick Jagger, and Elvis Costello.

As his career progressed into his senior years, he used his songwriting talents to voice his political views. In tandem with the name of his original group, the Equals, Eddy preaches equality.

He is missed in England and it would not be a stretch to hear one of his British fans making the plea, "**Baby Come Back**."

 BABY COME BACK

Open your smartphone camera & scan this QR code to listen to the song.

LOST IN THE INVASION

Aired in July 2005

In 1961 a fourteen-year-old girl, with a voice that you would associate with someone ten years older, hit the British pop charts with a bang with two of her first three recordings going to #1.

Given her age, you would think that she would be a "can't miss" in America with the British Invasion just around the corner. Unfortunately, this did not happen.

*****

The obvious richness and power of her voice resulted in this girl from London signing a recording contract with Columbia EMI in the UK.

Under the guidance and arrangements of Norrie Paramor, she hit the British pop scene in 1961 with three successful recordings in a row – "Don't Treat Me Like A Child" (#3), "You Don't Know" (#1), and "Walkin' Back To Happiness" (#1). Amazingly, only "Walkin' Back To Happiness" made the Billboard pop charts in the U.S. Even at that, it only held the 100th position for one week.

Despite a career on the rise, she could not compete with the English groups who excelled in North America during the British Invasion of the mid-60s.

As the young singer's pop career faded, she took every opportunity to become a blues artist. Today she is still going strong and is recognized in Europe in jazz and gospel circles.

In August of 1987 she became a committed Christian and now devotes herself mainly to her gospel outreaches, having completed 42 years of touring in show business at the end of 2002. However, she occasionally pops up on TV shows and radio programs and intends to continue recording.

Her early singles still give testimony to her splendid voice. Included in this group of recordings is her last Top 10 hit on the British charts that got some airplay in Canada, primarily in Toronto.

The singer was Helen Shapiro who was only sixteen years old when this last Top 10 came out in 1962. The song was about a teenage girl rebounding from a romance gone wrong, outlining how she was moving forward, and responding to the wrong that had been done to her with the attitude of **"I Don't Care."**

 I DON'T CARE

Open your smartphone camera & scan this QR code to listen to the song.

THE GROUP WITH THE GIRL DRUMMER

Aired in June 2002

One-hit wonders have been a source of fascination on *Treasure Island Oldies* since its inception. Many of these hits occurred during the teenage days of the baby boomers. Thanks to the Beatles and the British Invasion, a number of British bands made their mark in this category in North America.

One such group earned their "fifteen minutes of fame" when they made the transition from combing hair to strumming guitars and generating a Top 10 hit.

*****

Despite being a full-time hairdresser in the north part of London, Martin Murray, a former skiffle guitarist, still had an itch to form a group and play beat music. The Beatles and other local groups had turned him on to this new sound and the fan appeal could not go unnoticed.

To Murray's credit, he took action and ran an ad in a music paper. A guitarist/keyboard artist by the name of Alan Ward promptly replied. With Ward on board and thanks to some friends, Murray was able to attract vocalist/pianist/guitarist Dennis D'Ell. Murray filled the two remaining positions in the group with a fellow hairdresser and her brother.

By mid-1963 the group was garnering favourable reviews from local pubs. It wasn't long before they were introduced to the songwriting team of Ken Howard and Alan Blaikley who offered to manage the band and hook them up with independent producer Joe Meek. Meek had worked wonders with Lonnie Donegan, Johnny Kidd & the Pirates, and the Tornadoes of "Telstar" fame.

Their debut record soared to #1 in the UK, Canada, and Australia and #5 on the U.S. Billboard pop charts in the fall of 1964. If you saw them perform, you never forgot them for their setup was different from other bands of the time. They had a very good-looking female drummer – Annie Lantree.

The name of the group was the Honeycombs, derived from Lantree's nickname of "Honey," and the fact that both she and Martin Murray were "combers," a slang expression for hairdressers.

Following the success of their debut record, they chose to go on a worldwide tour instead of staying home and establishing themselves more on the UK charts. Unfortunately, their subsequent releases never measured up to their driving, upbeat hit, "**Have I The Right?**".

 HAVE I THE RIGHT?

Open your smartphone camera & scan this QR code to listen to the song.

ONE-HIT WONDER AT FOURTEEN

Aired in January 2003

The British Invasion of the mid-60s resulted in many #1 hits on the U.S. Billboard charts. But, do you recall the most successful #1 hit from Britain in the 50s?

It was recorded in 1958 on Capitol Records by a fourteen-year-old boy from London who became a one-hit wonder.

*****

In 1957 a young singer with a high-pitched voice and no musical training came to the forefront after successfully auditioning for *London's Radio Show*. He went on and made the most of an opportunity to record a Geoff Love adaptation of a traditional Afro-American gospel song.

The recording sold moderately well in England. However, it was embraced by North Americans and remained on the Billboard pop charts for 19 weeks and in the #1 position for 4 weeks – making it the most successful record by a British performer in North America in the 50s.

The young singer's rise to fame was so dramatic that he left school and his dad gave up his sales management job to become his son's manager.

The boy went on to make more pop/gospel recordings such as "Joshua," "The Gospel Train," and "I Gotta Robe," but none of these or other recordings for Roulette Records ever made the Billboard charts.

Some say that his dad's refusal to allow his son to travel and tour the United States while he was hot was a big mistake and cost the boy his career Stateside.

While walking down memory lane and listening to this song, it is not uncommon to mistake this one-hit wonder for a girl, given his high-pitched voice and his name, Laurie London.

Back in 1958, his dad would have been the first to tell you that **"He's Got The Whole World (In His Hands)."**

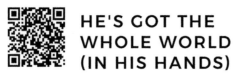

HE'S GOT THE WHOLE WORLD (IN HIS HANDS)

Open your smartphone camera & scan this QR code to listen to the song.

THE SCOTTISH LASS WITH CLASS

Aired in January 2003

There are a number of recording artists in the 50s and 60s that can attribute their recording success to the discovery and public acceptance of the B side of a label pressing.

In the case of a Scottish lass from Glasgow, a B side discovery in 1967 garnered this artist international recognition and critical acclaim.

*****

Marie McDonald McLaughlin Lawrie was fourteen years old when she was discovered singing with the Gleneagles in a small Glasgow nightclub. After numerous rejections, she eventually came up with a new name that was based on an American expression and a cartoon comic strip. Her new name – simply "Lulu."

The Gleneagles became Lulu And The Luvvers and made the British Top 10 in 1964 with their first recording, a cover version of the Isley Brothers' "Shout."

Lulu's biggest recording, of course, was the #1 smash hit "To Sir With Love." The song was released by Epic Records in North America in June of 1967, but what a lot of people don't know is that it was on the B side as the record company went with "The Boat That I Row" on the A side, a Neil Diamond composition that had made Top 10 in the UK.

Thanks to American disc jockeys who preferred the flipside, the film theme entered the Billboard Hot 100 in September and began its meteoric rise to the top of the charts by late October. This set the stage for a long career in radio, on TV, and in the theatre, as well as a span of 18 years on the U.S. Billboard pop charts.

One of Lulu's most prolific records that demonstrated the emotion in her voice came out in North America in late December of 1969, a ballad that was covered by Aretha Franklin in 1972.

Listening to this song, it is fair to speculate whether it was about her being head-over-heels in love with Maurice Gibb of the Bee Gees whom Lulu married in 1969 at the age of 20 - **"Oh Me, Oh My (I'm A Fool For You Baby)."**

 OH ME, OH MY (I'M A FOOL FOR YOU BABY)

Open your smartphone camera & scan this QR code to listen to the song.

AN IDENTITY CRISIS
Aired in April 2012

Fooling people on April Fool's Day is one thing, but fooling the music public for a whole recording career is another. But that's what happened in the late 60s in England, and that deception made its way to North America as well.

*****

The recording artist in question was born in Exeter, Devon, England in 1942 and had some modest regional success with various groups in the mid to late 60s.

An accomplished singer, he became a much sought after lead vocalist studio musician and would go on to have several hit songs under different group names.

In fact, in the spring of 1970, he had four hits on the Billboard Hot 100 under four different group names – Brotherhood of Man, Edison Lighthouse, White Plains, and the Pipkins, a duo group. The Brotherhood of Man release, "United We Stand," and the White Plains record, "My Baby Loves Lovin'," hit the Billboard charts in the U.S. on the same day – April 18, 1970. The Edison Lighthouse hit, "Love Grows (Where My Rosemary Goes)," came out in late February of 1970. The Pipkins' "Gimme Dat Ding" made it onto the charts in May of that year and went Top 10, peaking at the #9 position.

Even more incredible is the fact that on February 26, 1970, our lead singer with the identity crisis became the first - and still the only - person to appear on BBC television's *Top Of The Pops* while fronting three different acts on the same episode of the show: Edison Lighthouse (who were #1 that week), White Plains, and Brotherhood of Man.

The lead singer with the highly successful "April Fool's" career was Tony Burrows who has also recorded as a session singer with Elton John, Cliff Richard, and James Last.

He is sometimes referred to as the "one-hit wonder five times over." That fifth tune is from 1974, when Burrows, like the name of this group, does a First Class job singing lead on "**Beach Baby**."

 BEACH BABY

Open your smartphone camera & scan this QR code to listen to the song.

AMERICANS DISCOVERED
IN ENGLAND

Aired in May 2012

Late in 1964, Los Angeles musicians John Walker and Scott Engel met drummer Gary Leeds, previously of the Standells, a group that would go on to have a hit with "Dirty Water."

Leeds had just come back from England where he had toured with P.J. Proby. Believing that Walker and Engel's Rock & Roll and R&B style would go well in London, he was able to persuade the duo to come to England with him and check it out. Financial backing for the trip came from Leeds' stepfather.

They left for England in February 1965. By August of 1965 they had made it onto the Top 10 in the UK, eventually going to #1. They hit #1 a second time in the UK in March of 1966.

*****

Their first #1 hit in England that made it onto the Billboard Hot 100 in the fall of 1965 was a cover version of Jerry Butler's "Make It Easy On Yourself."

Their second #1 hit was also a cover, this time of a Frankie Valli record that failed to make the pop charts in North America. This UK #1 made it onto the Billboard charts in April of 1966 and went to the 13th position.

This was quite a feat, given the fact that the group was right in the midst of the British Invasion.

The trio called themselves the Walker Brothers because they liked the name. Scott Engel changed his name to Scott Walker, and Gary Leeds to Gary Walker. John Walker had actually been born John Maus – he changed his last name to Walker in his teens.

It's ironic that three unrelated American artists would have to travel to the UK to release some records and get discovered in order to get national recognition in their homeland. Who says, **"The Sun Ain't Gonna Shine (Anymore)"**.

Open your smartphone camera & scan this QR code to listen to the song.

IT'S ALL ABOUT TIMING?

Aired in January 2014

In reliving our pasts by attending concerts of artists we grew up with in the 50s, 60s, and 70s, we are sometimes "blown away" by their performances. It's like time stood still.

One reunited group from the 60s certainly falls into this category. This group also holds the unique distinction of having one of their most popular records make it onto the Billboard Hot 100 fourteen months after they had disbanded.

*****

This group has been referred to as one of the most underrated acts who were part of the original British Invasion. Their recent resurgence that included touring the UK, the U.S., Sweden, Denmark, Finland, Holland, and the Philippines supports this claim. In 2013 they released a new live album complementing their continual demand for appearances on U.S. network television shows and radio sessions. Recognition for dues paid.

Many believe that the secret to this group's current success was the reuniting of its two leaders – lead singer Colin Blunstone and singer/songwriter and organ/piano virtuoso Rod Argent.

The group's breakout record in 1964, "She's Not There," paved the way for touring in the United States.

In 1965, "Tell Her No," penned by Argent, went Top 10 in North America (#6) even though it failed to make the Top 40 in the UK.

In 1967 the group signed with CBS Records and produced an album titled *Odessey* and *Oracle*. The album was released in April of 1968 and sold poorly. Ironically, it was subsequently ranked #100 on *Rolling Stone's* list of the 500 greatest albums of all time.

What is even more ironic is that the group broke up in December of 1967 and ended up with a Top 10 hit on the Billboard Hot 100 (#3) in February of 1969 some fourteen months later, thanks to a release of a single from that ill-fated album.

Also written by Argent and beautifully sung by Blunstone, the two original members of the Zombies, you can only bow to this song, **"Time Of The Season."**

 TIME OF THE SEASON

Open your smartphone camera & scan this QR code to listen to the song.

GREAT DISAPPEARING
ACTS

The title of this chapter refers to the Rock & Roll artists who were only able to achieve national Top 40 status once throughout their career and were hence classified as one-hit wonders.

Truth be known, one-hit wonders were not uncommon during the Rock & Roll years of the 50s, 60s, and 70s. To get a record on the national charts was a feat in itself – sustaining the momentum with a follow-up hit or, in the case of groups, keeping personnel together and in line, was something else.

The following ten moments in time feature some extraordinary artists who were fortunate to have their "fifteen minutes of fame" thanks to national acceptance of one of their recordings.

THE PARTY'S OVER

Aired in February 2007

Thanks to parental encouragement, persistence, and a little bit of luck in the form of a deejay flipping a record over to play the B side, a 21-year-old singer found herself in the spotlight in 1962.

*****

As she was growing up in Macon, Georgia in the 40s and 50s, a little girl took a liking to producing musical sounds. Her parents also supported her by giving her guitar and organ lessons. After completing high school, she won a musical scholarship that eventually led to a B.SC. degree in musical composition.

As a result of spotting her on a television show in Wilmington, Delaware, Al Silver of Herald Records offered the young performer an opportunity to record a couple of her own tunes. Unfortunately, both efforts bombed ... but thanks to Bob Marcucci's Philadelphia-based Chancellor label, she was given a third chance in 1962.

The A side of the release was a song called "Disappointed." Unfortunately, it lived up to its title as it disappointed its listeners. However, thanks to some deejay who flipped the record over and played the B side, our new young artist had a hit on her hands overnight.

The song was a raunchy rocker that went to #3 on the R&B charts and to #5 on the Billboard Hot 100. Sadly, the young singer was never able to follow up the success with another hit. She even tried changing her name a couple of times ... to Joy Dawn on the Swan label and Sherry Pye on Match Records.

According to some reports, she disappeared from public view and went off into the wild, writing a Rock & Roll operetta, poetry, and plays.

It's a true lost treasure, one that allowed singer Claudine Clark to enjoy her time under the "**Party Lights**."

 PARTY LIGHTS

Open your smartphone camera & scan this QR code to listen to the song.

GOT A HIT - NEED A GROUP
Aired in November 2015

In the mid to late 60s, we were "blessed," and we say this loosely, with "bubblegum" music. Groups like the Ohio Express and the 1910 Fruitgum Company may come to mind.

One such group that fell into the "bubblegum" category was a studio concoction that became a one-hit wonder.

*****

According to an early 1969 article in *Cashbox*, a Welsh newspaper called *Mining News* had mentioned the hard-rock activities of a group of coal miners who would dig by day and play Rock & Roll by night.

The story goes on to describe a London, England club owner rushing to Wales and descending "18,372,065 feet beneath the surface" to sign the group.

Quite a story, especially since the *Cashbox* article was a complete fabrication, a publicity stunt, and one that came to pass after a group of American studio musicians got together in March of 1969 to produce what turned out to be a hit record.

With Robert Spencer, former member of the R&B group, the Cadillacs, singing lead and Joey Lavine of Ohio Express and Reunion fame on backup vocals, the song reached the #12 position on the Billboard Hot 100 and was a popular choice at clubs and parties throughout the U.S. and Canada.

A touring group was formed later to meet the demand for public appearances. These "bubblegumming" coal miners were known as Crazy Elephant, a group who brought teenagers to their feet with the hard-driving beat of "**Gimmie Gimmie Good Lovin'**."

GIMME GIMME
GOOD LOVIN'

Open your smartphone camera & scan this QR code to listen to the song.

THE NAME'S NOT QUITE THE SAME
Aired in November 2001

It was not uncommon in the 50s and 60s for artists to cover other artists' material and release it on a different record label at the same time as the original.

Some examples are Andy Williams covering Charlie Gracie's song "Butterfly" in 1957, which ended up being a #1 hit for both artists; Wayne Newton and Vic Dana releasing remakes of Vaughan Monroe's 1949 hit "Red Roses For A Blue Lady" in February of 1965; and Dante And The Evergreens and the Dyna-sores successfully charting with their cover versions of "Alley Oop," a #1 hit for the Hollywood Argyles – all of these versions were introduced on different labels in late May/early June of 1960.

The above-cited cases took place in North America. However, it occurred quite often overseas with many English artists covering U.S. performers.

In June of 1960, the reverse occurred, with an American artist covering an English singer's song. The catalyst in this instance was a movie.

*****

One of the great record producers of the late 50s and early 60s was Snuff Garrett. In 1960, while he was at Liberty Records, an English movie titled *Circus Of Horrors* was causing quite a stir. More importantly to Snuff, it had a very catchy song attached to it.

Without delay he called singer James "Buzz" Cason into the studio to cover the song so he could get it out on the street fast. Legend has it that it was recorded on Saturday, mastered and pressed on Sunday, and was in the stores on Monday.

By the time Buzz Cason finished recording the song, he had a "new" name, Garry Miles. The name was a direct rip-off from the name of the original British recording artist, Garry Mills.

Both records hit the Billboard pop charts on June 20, 1960. The original, Garry Mills' version, stayed on the charts for 11 weeks, peaking at the 26th position. Garry Miles' rendition proved to be the more successful of the two, lasting 13 weeks on the charts and peaking at the 16th position.

Garry Miles, or should I say Buzz Cason, went on to produce the Crickets and Buddy Knox for the Liberty label and to provide a lot of background vocals for the likes of Bobby Vee, Walter Brennan, and Jackie DeShannon. He was also the lead singer for Brenda Lee's backup band, the Casuals.

Sounding somewhat similar to Frankie Avalon's 1959 "Bobby Sox To Stockings" is Garry Miles' cover version of **"Look For A Star."**

 LOOK FOR A STAR

Open your smartphone camera & scan this QR code to listen to the song.

COVERED AND FORGOTTEN
Aired in April 2001

In the early days of Rock & Roll many of the so-called hits were remakes of standards from the 30s and 40s. A classic example of this is the 1959 hit "Smoke Gets In Your Eyes" by the Platters, a tune that was a #1 hit for Paul Whiteman's Orchestra in 1934.

Probably the greatest remake artist of the Rock & Roll era was Johnny Rivers who was extremely successful at remaking records originally done by a variety of popular performers. His timing for people wanting to hear that familiar tune again was impeccable.

*****

Rivers recorded for twelve different labels from 1955-1964 prior to his smash debut with Imperial Records. It took him eleven years to become an overnight success!

His first two hits were Chuck Berry numbers, "Memphis" and "Maybelline." He went on to do remakes of Leadbelly's "Midnight Special," a tune that was popularized by Paul Evans in 1960; the Kingston Trio's "Where Have All The Flowers Gone"; Buck Owens' country hit "Under Your Spell Again"; the Four Tops' "Baby I Need Your Lovin'"; the Miracles' "Tracks Of My Tears"; and the Beach Boys' "Help Me Rhonda," to name a few.

However, his third hit strayed from his formula of remaking a hit by a well-known artist. It was a cover of a one-hit wonder from 1960, written and recorded for Rita Records by a relatively unknown singer from Mississippi by the name of Harold Dorman. Rivers released his cover version of the song in 1964. It stayed 11 weeks on the Billboard Hot 100 and surpassed the original by peaking at the #9 position.

Harold Dorman was 34 years old when he wrote and recorded this song in February of 1960. Although it only managed to get to the 21st position, it stayed on the pop charts for 19 weeks, which was quite a feat for a first-timer.

Being so well received for such a long period of time made Dorman feel that he was on a "**Mountain of Love.**"

 MOUNTAIN OF LOVE

Open your smartphone camera & scan this QR code to listen to the song.

THE PERENNIAL SUMMER SONG
Aired in June 2003

Summer and the things associated with it, such as the beach, drive-ins, and parties, proved to be the perfect backdrop to many successful tunes penned in the late 50s and early 60s.

In 1959, a chance meeting with Pat Boone on the steps of a church one Sunday paved the way for a one-hit wonder that has become a perennial favorite in welcoming the summer.

*****

In 1956 a nineteen-year-old moved from the Midwest to New York City and began studying singing, cutting demos, and appearing on local TV shows whenever possible. One Sunday afternoon on the steps of a church, he met Pat Boone, then at the height of stardom.

Boone befriended the eager and talented teenager and gave him a list of people in the business who could help him. This led to his hooking up with Marty Mills who became his manager. A contract with Kapp Records followed.

On June 29, 1959, the teenager's self-penned summer song debuted in North America and remained on the Billboard pop charts throughout the summer for 13 straight weeks.

Despite a massive tour of the UK – replacing the recently deceased Rock & Roll headliner Eddie Cochran – none of the young man's subsequent releases ever received much airplay and his career soon faded, putting him in the one-hit wonder category.

However, he continued to write, with his "Turn Down Day" becoming a sizable hit for the Cyrkle in 1966, and his "Almost There" appeared in the 1964 movie *I'd Rather Be Rich*. A version of "Almost There" by Andy Williams also hit the chart in the same year.

What is unique about his 1959 one-hit wonder amongst all the other one-hit wonders is the fact that it is not a lost treasure. Each year, as summer approaches, this joyous tune rides the turntables.

Maybe best described as the man who puts full value in going to church, Jerry Keller continues to be recognized for his seasonal anthem, **"Here Comes Summer."**

 HERE COMES SUMMER

Open your smartphone camera & scan this QR code to listen to the song.

A WAIL OF A TUNE
Aired in March 2006

In the late 40s and early 50s, the crying balladeering style of Johnnie Ray captured the hearts of many teenagers throughout the world. In England he was once chronicled as the "Prince Of Wails" by a local punster.

Other artists tried copying Ray's style and had some success. One such artist reached the #5 position on the Billboard pop charts in 1960 with his first and only successful release.

*****

In 1958, after building up quite a local reputation wailing at churches and community functions, a sixteen-year-old boy, accompanied by his uncle, headed to New York City to try his luck at the amateur talent shows held at the Apollo Theatre.

That's all this young artist needed as he went on to win the renowned contest for four consecutive weeks. His name was Jimmy Charles.

Subsequently, Charles' uncle hooked him up with Phil Medley, an accomplished songwriter and musician who liked the wailing style and had him cut a demo.

The demo was then heard by Bill Lashley, one of the chief honchos at Promo Records. From there came a recording contract, a release of the record, and a meteoric rise to the #5 position on the Billboard Hot 100 in September of 1960.

Like the title of the tune, the chances of this happening for a young artist like Jimmy Charles on his first go-round were "**A Million To One**."

 A MILLION TO ONE

Open your smartphone camera & scan this QR code to listen to the song.

A BRUSH WITH SINATRA

Aired in March 2007

On Christmas Day in 1996, a heart attack took the life of a 67-year-old Philadelphian who had begun making a name for himself in music back in the early 50s.

Although he only received national prominence for a fleeting moment in 1956 with a record that reached the 12th position on the Billboard pop charts, he was unique among the one-hit wonders in that he caught the attention of Frank Sinatra.

*****

In 1955 Sinatra released the now-classic "Learnin' The Blues." It went to the #1 position and remained on the pop charts for 21 weeks. However, Sinatra's version was a remake of the original tune performed by Joe Valino, an unknown singer from South Philadelphia.

According to Valino, Sinatra heard him perform "Learnin' The Blues" while working with him at the 500 Club in Atlantic City. Sinatra complimented Valino on his singing ability, said that he would remember his name, and proclaimed that if he could do something for the singer, he would.

In Valino's words, "And he did it to me. I was in Detroit when I got the call. Somebody called and said, 'Sinatra's recording your record, right now!'"

Valino repaid the tribute by covering Sinatra's "Not As A Stranger." Unfortunately, sales were mild.

But thanks to his great voice, RCA got wind of Valino and signed him up to their subsidiary label, Vik. It was on this label that he recorded a stirring ballad that remained on the Billboard pop charts for 20 weeks in 1956, peaking at the 12th position. The record would go on to chart big in England and in some regions of Europe.

Unfortunately, follow-up recordings failed to maintain the momentum and Valino was soon forgotten.

Despite the lack of stardom, he continued to perform in nightclubs and cut albums throughout the 60s and 70s. The 80s brought on health problems – strokes, heart attacks, and bypass surgery. A fatal heart attack occurred on Christmas Day in 1996 in his mother's home.

During his battles with his health, he was quoted as saying, "I'll get it back. I just won't stop. I'll just play the piano in the bars until I get my bearings back. I'll sing again. I'm strong, thank God. I'm ready."

Today his hit record is rarely played and has become a lost treasure. We can only hope that Joe's passing resulted in him finding his "**Garden Of Eden**."

 GARDEN OF EDEN

Open your smartphone camera & scan this QR code to listen to the song.

THE TWO-TIME ONE-HIT WONDER
Aired in March 2007

Many of the artists associated with one-hit wonders were successfully involved in other areas of the music scene for long periods of time. Songwriters and producers often fall into this category.

In fact, there is one songwriter/producer who is considered unique in the annals of Rock & Roll for he is known as a "two-time one-hit wonder."

*****

This "two-time one-hit wonder" was too busy to enjoy his second one-hit wonder of 1968 as he had just penned "Mary In The Morning" for Al Martino, which reached #27 in late 1967, and was in the midst of a deal to produce Gene Pitney and some other acts.

When his record "Cinnamon" took off, he had his brother, who was part of his band, front the tune on the road. His logic was this: "Hey, there were three different touring versions of the Crystals, and two different versions of the Drifters, so it seemed like a good idea to have two different Dereks." Besides, his brother was named Derek.

Yes, his 1968 hit, "Cinnamon" by Derek (his stage name at the time) was his second one-hit wonder.

This multi-talented man was born in Scotland in 1945, moved to Goderich, Ontario in Canada in 1952, and then on to Cleveland in 1960. He became the music director for the Partridge Family and for the cartoon show, *Cat-nooga Cats*.

In addition to working with Gene Pitney, he produced recordings for Mae West and wrote tunes for Bette Midler, Reba McIntyre, and Elvis Presley.

Up until his untimely death from a heart attack in March of 1993, at age 48, our singer/songwriter continued to make public appearances and be involved in production work.

He spent his last ten years in Nashville, primarily writing, and had twenty songs on the country charts, most notably, "I'm Drinkin' Canada Dry" (Burrito Brothers) and "Fire In The Sky" (Wright Brothers).

However, he would have been the first to tell you that the reason that he is still remembered is because of his first one-hit wonder that debuted on the Billboard Hot 100 five years earlier in 1963.

The song was credited and recorded by him under his real name, Johnny Cymbal. Assisting him was bass vocalist Ronnie Bright, a member of the Valentines and a key contributor on **"Mr. Bass Man."**

 MR. BASS MAN

Open your smartphone camera & scan this QR code to listen to the song.

A NAME CHANGE SHOULD DO IT

Aired in November 2006

One-hit wonders remain a phenomenon of the 50s and 60s that many fans of Rock & Roll music find fascinating. Some argue that the artists and groups credited with these hits actually typified this era that featured constant interchange and disbanding of groups in addition to the fickle nature of the teenage audience. In fact, artists like Chuck Berry, Elvis, the Beatles, and the Rolling Stones became exceptions to the rule.

Sometimes, however, the one-hit wonder status was given out erroneously as artists or groups would often record under a different name in order to project a different style or crack a different segment of the market.

Such was the case with the singing group, the Little Dippers.

*****

In late 1959 the Little Dippers recorded the song "Forever," their only hit. It was released on University Records in January of the following year and reached the #9 position on the Billboard pop charts weeks later.

A dreamy ballad, it was on every teenager's make out list. Today the record is a collector's item.

The voices heard on "Forever" were those of a prominent artist and her behind-the-scenes singers whose previous credits included accompaniments for the likes of

Eddie Arnold, Chet Atkins, Brook Benton, the Browns, Perry Como, Floyd Cramer, Skeeter Davis, Red Foley, Connie Francis, Lorne Greene, Brenda Lee, Roy Orbison, and Jim Reeves.

They also began recording for themselves in 1951. Back then and during their studio session work, they were known as the Anita Kerr Singers. But as the Little Dippers they will be known **"Forever."**

 FOREVER

Open your smartphone camera & scan this QR code to listen to the song.

A PROFITABLE JOKE
Aired in April 2008

A candid interview with an artist from a group that was a one-hit wonder in the mid-70s produced this quote from the artist: "Basically, the song started as a joke and that joke is still making us money to this very day."

That "joke" made the Top 10 and peaked at the #9 position on the Billboard Hot 100 in September of 1977.

*****

In the mid to late 70s, Disco music was king. However, during that period, funk music and up-tempo R&B had a following as well.

That proved to be a good thing for songwriter/musicians Johnny Townsend and Ed Sanford, and for aspiring classical guitarist Steven Stewart.

According to Townsend, one morning Ed Sanford started complaining to Steven Stewart that he should forget classical music and concentrate on music that would make him some money.

With that, Stewart picked up his guitar and created a cool R&B rhythm and remarked that "anybody can write that crap."

Townsend immediately went to the piano and embellished on Stewart's creation. He soon added a title from a poem that Sanford had written in college, as it was a fit for the chorus idea he had for the song.

What started out as a joke and a challenge resulted in a hit record. Where there's smoke, there's fire. In this case, for the Sanford Townsend Band, it was "**Smoke From A Distant Fire.**"

SMOKE FROM A DISTANT FIRE

Open your smartphone camera & scan this QR code to listen to the song.

THE HIT
(RE)MAKERS

Being first out with an original release did not guarantee success during the early days of Rock & Roll. In fact, limited label and promotional support proved to be the downfall for many original recordings.

It was not uncommon, especially in the late 50s, for recordings to be released by several different artists at the same time, with each record label vying for top status.

There is also one other thing to note - a good song passes the test of time.

The following ten moments in time expose some of these original recordings with a focus on their timing of release and their road to becoming national hits.

BLENDING BLUE-EYED SOUL
WITH BEACH MUSIC
Aired in June 2017

A group formed in Portsmouth, Virginia in 1959 became very successful in crossing blue-eyed soul with the beach music of the Carolinas.

Their biggest hit was "What Kind Of Fool Do You Think I Am" in August of 1969. It was a remake of a song that was originally released by an Atlanta R&B group known as the Tams. Today this song is recognized as a Carolina beach music classic.

However, it was this blue-eyed soul group breakout record in January of 1969 that really got them started. It too was a cover version of a song written by another R&B performer from the 60s.

*****

During the early 60s the group got to share the stage and rub shoulders with the likes of Fats Domino and other 50s R&B legends. Their popularity grew by leaps and bounds with young Southern beachgoers.

They soon began filling seaside resorts along the Atlantic seaboard. During this era Bo Didley cut one of his finest albums, *Bo Didley's Beach Party*, live from Myrtle Beach, South Carolina.

At these Atlantic seaboard sessions, our blue-eyed soul group started performing an obscure song originally written and performed in 1965 by singer/songwriter Maurice Williams (of "Little Darlin'" and "Stay" fame). This song broke open the floodgates for them.

Audiences loved their rendition, so the group added it to their repertoire after getting numerous requests from a casino crowd.

They played it for a couple of years in fairly straightforward fashion and actually grew tired of the song, dropping it from their set at one point in 1968. By sheer happenstance, on a whim, at one performance that year, someone shouted the request and the leader of the group decided to add something different to make it more interesting for the band. They simply added a polka beat, and the audience went wild.

Accounts vary as to whether the band recorded this new version as an experiment the very next day, or as many as two or three days later. At a studio in Norfolk, Virginia, they pressed a few hundred copies of their new rendition and went around offering the pressings to record stores in the Norfolk area.

That group who took yet another Maurice Williams' song to chart success was Bill Deal & The Rhondels. The song? "**May I.**"

 MAY I

Open your smartphone camera & scan this QR code to listen to the song.

A BEATLES NON-RELEASE

Aired in November 2002

Not only did the Beatles lead the British Invasion, they also were responsible for creating one-hit wonders in North America. One such wonder was a songwriting/vocal duo from Bristol, England who made the U.S. Billboard pop charts early in 1966 with a song written by John Lennon and Paul McCartney but never released as a single by the Beatles.

The songwriting talent of the Bristol duo far exceeded their ability to sustain national attention as performers. In fact, it was their songwriting talent that was responsible for future one-hit wonders.

*****

Late in 1965, Beatles' producer George Martin heard a demo by countrymen Roger Greenaway and Roger Cook and decided to record them in the style of pop duos of the time like Chad & Jeremy and Peter & Gordon. Their initial release was a song written by Lennon & McCartney from the Beatles' *Rubber Soul* album. It was an instant hit Stateside and well received back home in England. British fans responded even more warmly to the duo's follow-up recording, "Lovers Of The World Unite."

By mid-1968, the two Rogers had stopped performing and recording and concentrated their efforts on composing, jingle-writing, and session work. This proved to be a wise move as many groups of the time were rewarded with hit records penned by them. Groups that benefited included the Fortunes who had "You've Got Your Troubles" and "Here Comes That Rainy Day Feeling Again"; the New Seekers with "I Like To Teach The World To Sing"; and the Hollies with "Long Cool Woman."

They also wrote tunes that made one-hit wonders out of Whistling Jack Smith ("I Was Kaiser Bill's Batman"); Edison Lighthouse ("Love Grows (Where My Rosemary Goes)"); and White Plains ("My Baby Loves Lovin'").

In 1971, the British Songwriters Guild voted Roger Greenaway and Roger Cook "Songwriters Of The Year" just five years after their recording of a well-recognized Beatles tune, a tune that the Beatles never released as a single in North America.

Better known back then as David & Jonathan, the two Rogers proved to be a pleasant surprise in 1966 with their version of "**Michelle**."

 MICHELLE

Open your smartphone camera & scan this QR code to listen to the song.

DON'T LET THE TITLE STOP YOU
Aired in May 2005

In the early to mid-60s there were a number of male/female singing duos that hit the Rock & Roll scene including Dale & Grace (with their #1 1963 hit "I'm Leaving It Up To You"); Paul & Paula (with "Hey Paula," a tune that went to #1 in the same year); Nino Tempo and April Stevens (with "Deep Purple," a remake of an old standard that also went to #1 in 1963); and, of course, Sonny & Cher in 1965 with their chart topper, "I Got You Babe."

However, in late November of 1964, a singing duo, who had paved the way in 1961 for other duos to follow, returned to the Rock & Roll charts by breaking one of the Ten Commandments.

*****

In 1961 this pop singing duo formed when two California-based high school kids got together to perform original compositions. The male and writer in the group was Dick St. John who soon teamed up with another student, Mary Sperling. Eventually, they ended up on the doorstep of Lama Records with one of the tunes that St. John had written.

With Sperling supplying some bizarre harmonies, St. John sang the melody, overdubbing a high falsetto to complete the record. Together, they performed the song on

American Bandstand and it soared to #2 in 1961. The record? "The Mountain's High."

One day in the summer of 1964, the couple were driving and listening to another recording from an album by the Newbeats who were enjoying current success with their hit record "Bread And Butter."

The couple decided to break one of the Ten Comandments and cover the Newbeats' record that they were listening to, doing it in a similar style to "The Mountain's High."

What resulted? Dick St. John and Mary Sperling, better known as Dick And Deedee, were back on the charts with **"Thou Shalt Not Steal."**

**THOU SHALT
NOT STEAL**

Open your smartphone camera & scan this QR code to listen to the song.

TABOO AT WEDDINGS
Aired in August 2019

In 1949 Eddie "Piano" Miller and Robert Yount co-wrote a song that would become extremely popular in the 50s and 60s, charting throughout these decades on both sides of the Atlantic.

Inspired by Jivin' Gene & The Jokers' 1960 version of this song, a young black singer had her arrangement released in 1962, and it became a crossover hit on both the R&B and Billboard pop charts in North America.

*****

In 1954, Ray Price and Kitty Wells' versions of this song went to #6 and #8, respectively, on the country charts; Patti Page put out a pop version that same year.

Other North American releases included the Everly Brothers in 1963, followed by Jerry Wallace in 1966 and Dean Martin in 1967.

In the UK, Engelbert Humperdinck's version went to the #1 position on the charts, remaining there for 6 straight weeks and denying the Beatles' "Penny Lane/Strawberry Fields Forever" the top spot. His version also went to #4 on the Billboard Hot 100.

In addition to this, Humperdinck's version became the highest selling single of 1967 in the UK, eventually becoming one of the best-selling singles of all time with sales of 1.38 million copies.

One of the most popular North American versions was a crossover record that went to #1 on the R&B charts and #8 on the Billboard Hot 100.

Performed by an artist who was comfortable doing pop, country, jazz, blues, or soul, it is a heartfelt ballad, but one that is taboo on wedding playlists. Why? You will get a pretty good idea when you hear the lyrics Esther Phillips sings in "**Release Me.**"

 RELEASE ME

Open your smartphone camera & scan this QR code to listen to the song.

IN BLACK AND WHITE

Aired in October 2007

Four years after the Beatles made their historic appearance on *The Ed Sullivan Show* in February 1964, a group hailing from Youngstown, Ohio exploded onto the Billboard pop charts with a Top 10 record.

The record was a remake of an Isley Brothers' tune that failed to chart back in 1962. Fortunately for the group, they picked the right moment in time to re-release it.

*****

The members of the group came from different bands and began gelling as a group playing in the Old Barn Bar in Youngstown, Ohio.

Although they were good enough to get studio time to record, things did not auger well for them initially. Vocalist and bass player Mel Pachuta summed up their frustration best. In an interview with *Discoveries'* Robert Hanley, Mel quipped, "We paid for the studio time and even paid for the records. And, damn, it took them like six months to get us the records." By then, the Shadows of Knight were well positioned on the Billboard Hot 100 with their version of "Gloria."

Once Tommy Shannenberger, a sales rep with Capitol Records, became their manager, things began to change.

They re-recorded, "Nobody But Me," an Isley Brothers record, and began getting attention on the black radio stations almost immediately because they were thought to be black. Once the stations realized they weren't black, they dumped the record.

However, by that time, the white stations had started playing the record and its popularity kept building and building. When February 3, 1968 rolled around, "Nobody But Me" was sitting at the #8 position on the Billboard Hot 100.

In promoting their hit single on tour, this group opened for the likes of Mitch Ryder And The Detroit Wheels, Paul Revere And The Raiders, Gary Puckett And The Union Gap, and Neil Diamond.

There was such a rush to get the record out into the market that Capitol spelled the group's name wrong on all the pressings. Looking back, I guess the group didn't mine too much – after all they were just ... Human Beinz ... and they had a hit single with **"Nobody But Me."**

 NOBODY BUT ME

Open your smartphone camera & scan this QR code to listen to the song.

ANSWERING THE ROLLING STONES

Aired in February 2003

In the late 50s and early 60s, music fans were introduced to "answer" records - songs that were sometimes a
parody or a sequel to recently established hits.

A few that come to mind are Jeanne Black's "He'll Have
To Stay" in 1960, the answer record to Jim Reeves' smash
hit of 1959/60, "He'll Have To Go"; Jody Miller's 1965
"Queen Of The House," the answer to Roger Miller's 1965
signature song "King Of The Road"; and Lesley Gore's
1963 "Judy's Turn To Cry," the follow-up record to her hit
"It's My Party."

In most cases these answer records usually came out a
few months after the success of the records they were emu-
lating. One grand exception to this rule was an answer
record that took eight years before it made it on the charts.
Recognized today as a core Rock & Roll record, it went all
the way to #1.

*****

By the mid-70s the Rolling Stones were well established
with seven #1 hits to their credit. In 1974 they put out a
tongue-in-cheek tribute to their love of music - "It's Only
Rock 'N Roll (But I Like It)."

The song stirred up the creative juices of Alan Merrill, a
band member of the Anglo/American group known as the
Arrows. Although he realized that the Rolling Stones
didn't really mean to be derogatory about the music of the

time, Merrill felt compelled to respond to the Stones' tune through song.

Most thought that Merrill's answer record was okay but wouldn't be a hit so it got lost on the B side of one of the Arrows' British singles in 1975. In the late 70s an all-girl band from the States, the Runaways, saw the Arrows performing this song on their TV show. A member of the Runaways subsequently called the group and asked for permission to record the song.

Unfortunately, the rest of the Runaways refused to record the song. The Runaways eventually broke up and the member with the eagerness to record the tune did so, releasing it in Holland in the early 80s. By 1982 she was back in America and had formed her own group. The group recorded the song again, only to be faced with contemporary hit radio stations saying it was too punk, and new wave stations feeling it was too rock.

But perseverance paid off. Being primarily a touring band, the group made the song their anthem and created such a demand that radio stations of all types were forced into playing it. By the week of March 20, 1982, this answer song was #1 on the Billboard Hot 100 and remained there for 7 straight weeks.

Riding the wave at the #1 position was Joan Jett & The Blackhearts, who were constantly encouraging their fans to "put another dime in the jukebox baby" because **"I Love Rock 'N Roll."**

 I LOVE ROCK 'N ROLL

Open your smartphone camera & scan this QR code to listen to the song.

A POLITICALLY CORRECT REMAKE

Aired in July 2005

From 1955 to 1959 the market share for Rock & Roll increased from 15.7% to 42.7%, making it the fastest grow- ing genre of music ever. However, in the late 50s an appetite for folk music started to evolve.

One of first nationally recognized groups for this type of music had the distinction of reissuing their version of a recording in 1959 that had been banned in Boston a decade earlier.

*****

Discovered in the spring of 1957 while performing at the Cracked Pot in Redwood City, California, a folk trio signed a contract drawn up on a table napkin by publicist Frank Werber.

One year later, after polishing their act and gaining popularity while touring the country, the three young men scored a #1 hit with their first charted recording on Bill- board, a rearrangement of a traditional American folk song written in 1868. The record? "Tom Dooley." (In 1868 it was originally written as "Tom Dula.") The group: the Kingston Trio.

They appeared on the Billboard pop charts seventeen times from 1958 to 1963 with such memorable tunes as "The Tijuana Jail," "The Reverend Mr. Black," and "Where Have All The Flowers Gone."

In the summer of 1959, they released a cover version of

a record about Boston's transit system. The original version by Will Holt had been hastily withdrawn from airplay a decade earlier due to its political overtones.

In the 1940s, the transit fare schedule in Boston was overly complicated. Fare increases were implemented by means of an "exit fare." Rather than modify all the turnstiles for the new rate, the transit authority just collected the extra money when passengers left the train. One of the key points of the platform of Walter A. O'Brien, a Progressive Party candidate for mayor of Boston, was to fight fare increases and make the fare schedule more uniform.

This became the backdrop for the text of the song written in 1948 by Jacqueline Steiner and Bess Lomax Hawes. It was one of seven songs written for O'Brien's campaign; each one emphasized a key point of his platform.

During the McCarthy era of the 1950s, the Progressive Party became synonymous with the Communist Party in the United States, and, since O'Brien was a Progressive, he was labeled a Communist. Although O'Brien was never on the Communist Party ticket, Holt's recording was removed from radio station playlists.

In 1959, the Kingston Trio released their version of the song. The name Walter A. O'Brien was changed to George O'Brien to avoid the problems that original artist, Holt, experienced. This resulted in the legend of "Charlie" on the "**M.T.A.**" being reborn.

 M.T.A.

Open your smartphone camera & scan this QR code to listen to the song.

UP-TEMPO FOLK
Aired in May 2011

In reminiscing about Rock & Roll and its early days, we sometimes forget that, concurrently, in the late 50s through to the mid-60s there was a strong and very success-ful folk music movement in North America. It included the likes of the Kingston Trio; Peter, Paul & Mary; Judy Collins; Glen Yarbrough (former lead of the Limeliters); and the Womenfolk.

For a two-week period in the winter of 1963, a folk trio from New York City controlled the #1 position on the Bill-board pop charts.

*****

The leader of this group of three was Erik Darling. Ear-lier in his career, Darling had been in the folk trio the Tarriers, who recorded "Cindy, Oh Cindy," a Top 10 hit in 1956. The record was released as being sung by Vince Martin & The Tarriers. As an aside, one of the other mem-bers in the group was future star actor, Alan Arkin.

The Tarriers soon disbanded, with Arkin returning to acting and Darling replacing the incomparable Pete Seeger in the Weavers from 1958 to 1962.

After listening to an old Gus Cannon folk blues song from 1929, Darling went out and recruited two of his friends: Bill Svanoe, a guitarist whose style was similar to Darling's, and Lynne Taylor, a jazz singer who had performed with Tommy Dorsey and Benny Goodman. The focus for this new trio was to record an updated and up-tempo version of Gus Cannon's song.

Darling wanted their version to be recorded with two 12-string guitars, but there weren't many to be found outside of pawn shops. Hence, he ordered two from the Gibson Guitar Company, and waited six months for them.

The record was a windfall for 79-year-old Cannon, who, in addition to earning publishing royalties from the re-release, was signed to a recording contract with Stax Records.

As fast as this group made it to #1 on the Billboard Hot 100 in 1963, they were gone, being only able to chart with two subsequent minor releases in the same year.

According to Darling, "We had a certain problem, in that the group was put together strictly for [remaking the song] ... there wasn't anything else that really fit ... we never did come up with anything that was remotely as good."

The trio, with a few personnel changes, stayed around until 1967. But we'll always remember Erik, Dave, and Lynne, better known as the Rooftop Singers, who created their own success in 1963 and were able to "**Walk Right In.**"

 WALK RIGHT IN

Open your smartphone camera & scan this QR code to listen to the song.

HATS OFF TO DEL
Aired in August 2007

Thanks to a fading popstar who knew talent when he saw it, a Los Angeles group got discovered, reissued a popular song, and ended up with a national hit that made it to #5 on the Billboard pop charts in the fall of 1969.

*****

By early 1969, a female singer by the name of Gayle McCormick and two members of her group, the Klassmen, had made the move to Los Angeles from St. Louis and hooked up with two more musicians.

While playing at the Rag Doll, a San Fernando Valley bar, they were heard by two early 60s pop stars, Del Shannon and Brian Hyland, who happened to be in the bar at the time.

Shannon really liked what he heard and invited the group to his home, which included a recording studio. It was his belief that the group would be perfect to do a more up-tempo, gritty remake of a successful Burt Bacharach, Mack David, and Barney Williams (aka Luther Dixon) hit composition that the Shirelles originally released in late 1961.

Shannon was well respected in the industry and was able to get all the major record labels to listen to the cover version he produced. ABC-Dunhill Records loved the sound and offered a contract.

Within nine months the group had a smash hit on their hands with national appearances on TV shows hosted by Ed Sullivan, Mama Cass, and Red Skelton.

Before a follow-up single could be produced and released, Shannon had left, conjecture being that the record label wanted to do its own thing with the group.

Sadly, within the next year, due to internal conflicts, the group disbanded despite reaching the charts two more times.

The group's rendition of Bacharach/David/Williams' composition has a fuller, more spirited sound, but does not get the airtime it richly deserves. When lead singer Gayle McCormick of the group Smith belts out the lyrics, you know that "**Baby It's You**."

 BABY IT'S YOU

Open your smartphone camera & scan this QR code to listen to the song.

REMAKING YOUR OWN RECORD
Aired in October 2000

You're probably familiar with the old adage that timing is everything. Well, this certainly holds true in the music industry.

In the case of records that were re-released, the timing of the re-release was a critical component to the record's renewed success. Often re-releases by the same artist were modest hits the second time around. However, this was not the case for a re-release by Tommy Edwards. In fact, he experienced the exact opposite.

* * * * *

Tommy Edwards was born in Richmond, Virginia. He moved to New York City in 1950 where he got a job singing demo records. Later in the year he signed on with MGM and recorded "The Morning Side Of The Mountain" which became a hit that summer.

Subsequently, he recorded a tune that went to #18 on the pop charts in 1951. What's interesting about the song that he chose to record was that the melody was written in 1912 by Charles Dawes who later became Vice-President of the United States under Calvin Coolidge, who was President from 1925-29. Songwriter Carl Sigman added the lyrics to Dawes' music in 1951, the year the song was first released.

By 1958, MGM was about ready to drop Edwards from their artist roster as his records were not selling. With one session left under his contract, Edwards was asked by MGM executive, Marty Craft, to remake his 1951 record, only this time in stereo.

Recording in stereo was the new thing at the time and some say this new technology saved Edwards' career.

Edwards' new up-tempo stereo version appealed to the MGM brass who decided to release it as a single. Amazingly, after 6 weeks on the Billboard Hot 100, it was sitting at the #1 position on September 29, 1958. By November it was #1 in the UK. A great ballad, it was also a hit for Cliff Richard in 1964.

Timing can be a wonderful thing. In the case of Tommy Edwards' 1958 re-release, you could say that "**It's All In The Game.**"

Open your smartphone camera & scan this QR code to listen to the song.

I DIDN'T
KNW
THAT

The axiom, "Truth is stranger than fiction," is well supported in the history of Rock & Roll.

The stories of how some songs came to be recorded and how some artists were discovered and matched with songs characterize the music scene of the 50s, 60s, and 70s.

The following ten moments in time explore some little-known facts behind some of the biggest records ever to make the national charts and the artists who made them famous.

GENE'S LOSS

Aired in January 2007

One of the more prolific singer/songwriters of the 60s and 70s was Joe South who, aside from writing a number of Top 10 hits for other artists, took center stage in 1968 when his song "Games People Play" won a Grammy for Song of the Year.

In his early days, he penned a tune and produced a demo with the hopes that Gene Pitney would listen to it and record it. Pitney never did.

*****

Joe South (real name Joe Souter) was born in 1940 and joined the Georgia Jubilee early in his career, performing with the likes of Jerry Reed, Ray Stevens, and other soon-to-be-discovered artists. In 1965 he asked one of the artists whom he had roomed with to record a demo of a tune he had written.

South's artist friend jumped at the opportunity and flew from Cincinnati, Ohio to Atlanta, Georgia to cut the demo.

The demo ended up at Columbia Records. Upon signing this unknown artist to a six-year deal, Columbia released the demo as a single. It went to #9 on the Billboard pop charts and #1 in Canada. It briefly made the singer into a teen idol, who went on from there to have a string of lesser hits and then crossed over to country in the early 80s.

That debut record about a boy from the "wrong side of the tracks" who is determined to make himself worthy of a girl of a higher class sounds similar in spots to Gene Pitney's "Twenty-Four Hours From Tulsa." As to the theme of the record, its lyrics parallel those of another hit record released twenty months earlier – "Midnight Mary" by Joey Powers.

Regardless, it was a huge hit for Billy Joe Royal, launching his career and being no longer **"Down In The Boondocks."**

Open your smartphone camera & scan this QR code to listen to the song.

FORESHADOWING FATE

Aired in January 2001

When it came to writing about love in the 60s, singers and songwriters did not shy away from voicing their opinions on what was allowed and wasn't allowed in relationships between two people.

In fact, a lot of their writings dealt with territorial issues and "crossing the line." Sometimes referred to as "warning records," songs like "Keep Your Hands Off My Baby" by Little Eva, "Don't Say Nothing Bad About My Baby" by the Cookies, and "My Boyfriend's Back" by the Angels fell into this category.

Early in 1966, a group from St. Louis hit the Billboard pop charts with their warning record. Ironically, the lyrics to this tune foreshadowed the fate of the group's lead singer seventeen years later.

*****

Peaking at #12 on the Billboard Hot 100 in 1966, this warning record proved to be the biggest hit for the group from St. Louis.

Tragically, the lead singer, Walter Scott, never got a chance to reunite with the group for its twentieth anniversary. Two days after Christmas in 1984, Scott (born Walter Notheis Jr.) went out for a jog, never to been seen again.

He was found dead just over three years later in April 1987, floating face-down in a reservoir. He had been tied up and shot in the chest, execution-style. Subsequently, his wife and her lover were indicted for murder.

His case was documented on Court TV's *Forensic Files*, HBO's *Autopsy 3: Voices From The Grave*, and on the March 23, 1999 episode of *The New Detectives: Case Studies in Forensic Science*.

Perhaps Scott should have taken heed to the words he sang back in 1966 when he was the lead singer for Bob Kuban And The In-Men: beware of "**The Cheater**."

 THE CHEATER

Open your smartphone camera & scan this QR code to listen to the song.

A LOVE BALLAD
Aired in February 2018

In paying our respects to the day the music died, we revisit a Buddy Holly number from his last recording session on October 21, 1958 at Decca Record's Pythian Temple Studios in New York City.

On that day Holly would record a beautiful love ballad that appeared on the album *The Buddy Holly Story, Vol II* released posthumously in March 1960.

*****

That recording session in New York featured Al Caiola on guitar, the same Al Caiola who, along with his orchestra, found success in late 1960 with "The Magnificent Seven," the theme instrumental for the movie of the same name that starred Yul Brenner. This instrumental was subsequently used in commercials for Marlboro cigarettes.

In addition to the love ballad recording, that session included two other Buddy Holly songs that became hits later on. The first was a Paul Anka composition, "It Doesn't Matter Anymore." It hit the charts on February 23, 1959 and would make it to the 13th position. The flipside, "Raining In My Heart," appeared on the charts on March 30.

However, that love ballad Holly co-wrote with Norman Petty did not get released as a single until after the album came out in 1960.

As a single, it was a hit in Britain in 1960, peaking at the 25th position on the pop singles chart but it failed to make it onto the Billboard Hot 100 that year. In 1988 it was re-released by MCA and made it to the 65th position on the UK charts.

In 1965 Peter & Gordon released their version of Holly's ballad during the British Invasion and it rose to the 14th position on the Billboard Hot 100.

Over the years numerous prominent artists, including Mickey Gilley, have recorded this song. Gilley's 1980 crossover version went to #1 on both the country charts in the U.S. and Canada, and to a respectable #66 on the Billboard pop charts.

The song is often heard at weddings. Many believe that Holly had actually written this song for his wife, Maria Elena Holly, as a wedding gift. However, a listing of producer Norman Petty's productions claims that Vi Petty, Norman's wife, recorded the first version of this song on June 4, 1958 - two weeks prior to Holly's first meeting with Maria.

Holly's biographer Bill Griggs points out that the melody borrows heavily from the gospel song "I'll Be All Right," a favorite of Holly's, and one that was played at his funeral.

A beautiful, heartfelt song that has passed the test of time, it is one that sums up Buddy Holly's belief about **"True Love Ways."**

 TRUE LOVE WAYS

Open your smartphone camera & scan this QR code to listen to the song.

DON'T LET FACT GET IN THE WAY OF A GOOD STORY

Aired in February 2014

It wouldn't be Christmas without the opportunity to view the perennial seasonal classic, *It's A Wonderful Life*, the 1948 movie starring Jimmy Stewart.

What many people don't know is that the picture actually bombed on the big screen when it first came out.

What is even more interesting is that fourteen years later, in 1962, Stewart had another picture that initially bombed and would go on to become recognized as one of the greatest westerns ever made. It even had a song associated with it.

*****

The movie, directed by the legendary John Ford, starred Jimmy Stewart along with John Wayne, Vera Miles, and Lee Marvin, who played the bad guy.

While the picture was being shot, a new hot pop artist was prepping to cut a song that was earmarked for the movie. The song went to #4 on the Billboard Hot 100 but was never released with the picture on the big screen.

As the story goes, during the recording session for this song, a friend of the artist's left the studio, went outside for a few minutes, and saw a marquee on a nearby building. The friend came back into the studio and broke the news about what he saw on the marquee — the movie was already out in the theaters.

To say that made the recording artist a little depressed is an understatement. "Here's a movie with Jimmy Stewart, Lee Marvin and John Wayne — and the song doesn't get into the movie," he said.

In the years to follow, the artist constantly heard two things from fans. Either they would say, "I thought your song was one of the best parts of the movie," or, "I was watching the movie on TV last night, and they cut your song out of it. They must have had to edit it for time."

Both sets of fans were wrong.

After years of gently setting his supporters straight, the artist gave up and let his fans believe what they wanted to believe. He was living up to a line with which every fan of *The Man Who Shot Liberty Valance* is quite familiar: "When the legend becomes fact, print the legend."

Throughout the years, wherever Gene Pitney performed, there was nothing too good for **"The Man Who Shot Liberty Valance."**

 **THE MAN WHO SHOT LIBERTY VALANCE**

Open your smartphone camera & scan this QR code to listen to the song.

ONLY IN AMERICA

Aired in April 2002

Racism has been a part of America's culture since its beginnings. It flourished in the distribution side of the music business in the early days of Rock & Roll, as large radio stations shied away from giving air time to black music, or "race records," as they were known at the time.

Thanks to some courageous people in the 50s such as deejays Alan Freed, Hunter Hancock, and Dewey Phillips, proper recognition of this music gradually spread across America. Positive public appeal resulted in increasing exposure of black artists and their music.

However, in the 50s and 60s this exposure was still guarded and racism remained present. In fact, it was because of this that a white group out of New York City ended up with a hit record that was key in sustaining their career.

*****

In February of 1962, Jay & The Americans hit the national charts by storm with a classic ballad, "She Cried." Soon after, lead singer John "Jay" Traynor left the group and was replaced by David Blatt.

A few months later, to accommodate the group, David Blatt changed his name to Jay Black. One day the new Jay and the rest of the Americans were in the offices of the famous songwriting team of Jerry Leiber and Mike Stoller, listening to a new recording by the Drifters entitled "Only In America."

Given their name and the tempo of the tune, Jay & The Americans thought that this song was a natural for them to record. Ironically, Leiber And Stoller were informed that Atlantic Records was not going to release the Drifters' version of the recording because they were not comfortable having a black group singing the line about getting "a break and maybe [growing] up to be President." They, the so-called "establishment," believed that many people in America felt the same way.

Faced with this, Leiber and Stoller made an arrangement with Atlantic to purchase the master tapes and had Jay & The Americans record over the original musical track. What resulted in the summer of 1963 was the group's first major hit with Jay Black as lead singer.

In reflecting on this turn of events, you might say that this could happen **"Only In America."**

 ONLY IN AMERICA

Open your smartphone camera & scan this QR code to listen to the song.

HOLLYWOOD AND SONG

Aired in June 2020

This moment in time spotlights one of Hollywood's film icons and a song he co-wrote in 1957 for a movie that he also co-wrote, starred in, and produced.

What is unique about the song is that the original Capitol release charted in both 1958 and 1962, appearing a combined 21 weeks on the Billboard pop charts.

*****

The movie featuring this song came out in 1958 and developed something of a cult following, and continued to play at drive-ins throughout the 70s and 80s in the Southeastern United States.

One of the roles in the movie was originally written for Elvis Presley with our film star personally delivering Presley a copy in Los Angeles. Presley was eager to play the role but negotiations broke down when Presley's manager, Colonel Tom Parker, demanded that Presley be paid a sum of money that was greater than the movie's entire budget.

As a result, Presley's part ended up going to the film icon's son, James, playing the role of the star's younger brother, which worked out well because of the family resemblance.

The film's plot revolved around the running of moonshine through the hills of Kentucky and Tennessee, culminating in a fatal last run and the death of Robin

Doolin, the son of Korean army veteran Lucas Doolin, played by Robert Mitchum.

That cult classic film was *Thunder Road*, a movie Mitchum once referenced as making more money for him than the previous fifty pictures he had been in.

For trivia buffs: second billing in the movie went to Gene Barry who soon afterwards became western hero "Bat Masterson" on TV.

So, fill up your tank, fasten your seat belts, and let the legendary Robert Mitchum transport you with "**The Ballad Of Thunder Road**."

THE BALLAD OF THUNDER ROAD

Open your smartphone camera & scan this QR code to listen to the song.

MONKEY BUSINESS

Aired in July 2017

Thanks to a little "monkeying around," an up-and-coming female artist led the way on a song that ended up being a big hit in 1967.

*****

A Northern Bluegrass band, the Greenbriar Boys, originally recorded a song that was included on their 1966 album, *Better Late Then Never.*

The song was written in 1965 by a singer/songwriter who won an Emmy for being part of a very popular comedy TV show. This soon-to-become TV star rushed through a version of the song in one of the episodes of this hit comedy show that aired in December of 1966.

However, it was in 1967 when a Los Angeles-based group released an arrangement that national attention followed. The song went to #13 on the Billboard Hot 100, #5 in New Zealand and regionally, #1 in Los Angeles, and #6 in Detroit.

Employing a more complex instrumental approach, the actual hit recording featured studio musicians and only one of the group's members, their lead singer. The group was known as the Stone Poneys and that lead singer was none other than Linda Ronstadt.

Now retired from singing, Ronstadt is recognized as a music icon, an artist who was equally adept in performing and recording in many genres, including rock, country, light opera, and even Latin. She has ten Grammy Awards, three American Music Awards, two Academy of Country Music Awards, and an Emmy to her credit.

With regards to Ronstadt's contribution to that 1967 hit record, the monkeying around with the arrangement met with the approval of its creator, former Monkee, Mike Nesmith. Nesmith is quoted as saying that Linda Ronstadt's performance of his song "infused it with a new level of passion and sensuality."

This is not surprising as Nesmith was also noted for following the beat of a "**Different Drum**."

 DIFFERENT DRUM

Open your smartphone camera & scan this QR code to listen to the song.

SKYLINE INSPIRATION

Aired in August 2015

When it came to weddings and social functions during the 70s, there was a record from the late 60s that consistently got the attendees up on the dance floor. It had an infectious beat with memorable lyrics that appealed to party-goers young and old.

*****

This song ranks right up there with other party records of the 60s such as "Let's Dance" by Chris Montez (1962), "The Locomotion" by Little Eva (1962), and the Beatles' version of "Twist And Shout" (1964) to name a few.

Written in 1968 by Tommy James, Ritchie Cordell, Bo Gentry, and Bobby Bloom, this foot stomper was completed in the studio before it had a title.

How the title came about was documented in a 1995 interview with Tommy James for *Hitch Magazine.*

True story: I had the track done before I had a title. I wanted something catchy like "Sloopy" or "Bony Maroney," but everything sounded so stupid. So Ritchie Cordell and I were writing it in New York City, and we were about to throw in the towel when I went out onto the terrace, looked up, and saw the Mutual of New York building (which has its initials [M.O.N.Y.] illuminated in red at its top). I said,

"That's gotta be it! Ritchie, come here, you've gotta see this!" It's almost as if God himself had said, "Here's the title." I've always thought that if I had looked the other way, it might have been called "Hotel Taft."

And thus was born one of the greatest audience participation records of all time. By Tommy James And The Shondells, this dancing tune could be classified as bankable – **"Mony Mony."**

Open your smartphone camera & scan this QR code to listen to the song.

FROM FILM & TV TO THE TOP TEN
Aired in November 2020

Recounting stories through song is a true art form. Artists like Johnny Cash with "A Boy Named Sue," Johnny Horton with "North To Alaska," and Jimmy Dean's "Big Bad John" were extremely successful in catching the interest of their listeners with their "story records."

In 1962, an artist, at the ripe old age of 67, made it to the #5 position on the Billboard Hot 100 with his story record.

*****

Our featured artist did not start recording music until 1960. But there is good reason for that. Prior to this, he had been immersed in the film and TV industry for 35 years. Born in 1894, he enlisted in the U.S. army and served in France during World War I.

After the war, he worked as a financial reporter in Boston, but with a goal of moving to Guatemala to grow pineapples. Somehow he ended up in Los Angeles and did quite well in the real estate market in the early 20s until the slump of 1925.

Penniless, he began taking parts as an extra in movies at $7.50 a day, just to make ends meet. However, this proved to be his calling. By 1940, this man had won three Oscars as Best Supporting Actor – in 1936, 1938, and 1940.

A number of roles in westerns during the 40s and 50s ensued and he was always recognizable whenever he appeared on the big screen. In the 50s he found himself doing TV as well, which he said he liked better because there were not "long layoffs between jobs."

In 1957 he struck gold with a leading role in a TV series that lasted seven seasons. The show was about a poor West Virginia family that relocated to a farm in Southern California. It is this show that Baby Boomers identify him with, despite the three Oscars he had previously won.

A consummate actor, he appeared in more than 230 film and TV roles during a career that spanned almost five decades. His name was Walter Brennan, a "real McCoy."

If he were around today to sum up his experience recording music, he probably would quote a line from *The Real McCoys* and say, "Dab burn it ... it was more fun than a three ring circus, Little Luke."

You can just picture Walter Brennan, a tremendous storyteller of song, out in the hay fields, looking around, and reminiscing about "**Old Rivers**."

 OLD RIVERS

Open your smartphone camera & scan this QR code to listen to the song.

A BALLAD FOR A BEAUTY

Aired in January 2009

One of the great teenage idols of the early 60s was Bobby Vinton. "Teenage Idol" may have been somewhat of a misnomer as Vinton was 27 years old when he entered and topped the Billboard Hot 100 in the summer of 1962 with "Roses Are Red," a tune that had been written by prominent singer/songwriter Paul Evans of "Seven Little Girls Sitting In the Back Seat" fame.

A year later Vinton remade a hit from the 50s and took it to #1 as well.

*****

Vinton, the son of a bandleader, formed his own band in high school. In 1960 he toured as the leader of the backing band for Dick Clark's *Caravan Of Stars*. Two years later he left the band to perform and record on his own. He never looked back. In addition to a successful singing career, he had his own musical variety TV series from 1975-78. It was during the 70s that he was affectionately dubbed "The Polish Prince" in America.

By January 1980, he had graced the U.S. pop charts 47 times, including ten Top 10 records and four #1s. Amazingly, three of his number ones records were remakes. The most interesting of the three was his second #1 recording, "Blue Velvet."

Many audiophiles will point out that "Blue Velvet" was recorded earlier by the Clovers. Indeed it was. In fact, the Clovers' version was released in 1955 and made it to the #14 position on the R&B charts.

However, the Clovers were not the first to record this tune. For that, we have to go back to 1951 and a young artist who was beginning to make a name for himself. His original version went to #18 on the pop charts that year. And that was just the beginning for this legendary music icon.

Although we rarely associate this 1951 release with its original singer, we sure get an appreciation of the talent of a young Tony Bennett as he describes a loved one wearing **"Blue Velvet."**

Open your smartphone camera & scan this QR code to listen to the song.

LOST IN THE
SHUFFLE

In the music industry it's often been said that timing coupled with a little bit of luck were the cornerstones for success.

Unfortunately, some artists and their releases were not blessed with either, experiencing poor promotion, unscrupulous management, and unforeseen competition.

The following ten moments in time explore recordings that are rarely heard today, some of which make you scratch your head as to why they were not big hits and mainstays in Rock & Roll history.

A FOOTNOTE IN POP HISTORY

Aired in January 2010

In this day and age, with the information overload that the Internet provides, you would think that it would be pretty simple to find out something about anybody, especially in the music industry.

But that is not the case regarding a young American female recording artist from the late 50s and early 60s who cut her teeth with the likes of legendary songwriters/lyricists duos Leiber & Stoller as well as Burt Bacharach & Hal David.

This Philadelphia-born artist had the looks and talent but failed to get the breaks, being successfully covered by Helen Shapiro in the UK and surpassed by Dionne Warwick Stateside.

Still, she is remembered by a few and her recordings have become sought-after collectibles.

*****

You would think that by signing with Kapp Records in 1961, and being able to record for Burt Bacharach and Hal David, that an artist would have it "made in the shade" as they would say back then.

But life is not always fair, and our talented artist who was once described as the diminutive gal with the big, big voice failed to achieve national stardom, barely qualifying as a footnote to a footnote in pop music history.

However, she did enjoy some success north of the border in Canada in 1962. That year she made it onto CHUM Radio, the top pop station in Toronto. In fact, her release made it to #9 on the CHUM Charts and remained on those charts for nine straight weeks. She also made it to #6 on the Vancouver charts.

In the U.S., this record peaked at #97 on Cashbox and bubbled under the Billboard Hot 100 at #117. However, she did enjoy some regional success, making it to the #2 position in Springfield, Massachusetts.

It's too bad that music executives who admired the talents of Philadelphia's Babs Tino failed to spend more time on her career in order to garner the national recognition she deserved. Any one of them would probably be willing to say the following to her: **"Forgive Me (For Giving You Such A Bad Time)."**

FORGIVE ME (FOR GIVING YOU SUCH A BAD TIME)

Open your smartphone camera & scan this QR code to listen to the song.

SHE SANG LIKE AN ANGEL
Aired in February 2010

In the spirit of Valentine's Day, our hearts go out to a female vocalist from the early 60s who blessed us with a beautiful ballad and subsequently slipped away into the sunset.

There were a number of great female artists tearing up the charts in the early 60s. We had the well-established Brenda Lee and Patsy Cline in the United States, Pat Hervey was making a name for herself in Canada, and across the Atlantic, Helen Shapiro was drawing a lot of attention in the UK.

Our forgotten artist was a native of San Diego and was discovered while working as a department store sales-woman. She made her one and only appearance on the charts in 1962.

*****

Although she only made it to the 61st position on the Billboard Hot 100, she remained on those charts for 9 weeks — quite an accomplishment for her, given that her release was on the small, independent Brent recording label.

The significance of this record was not the fact that it made it onto the Billboard pop charts; it was the record's ability to be rediscovered from time to time over the decades that followed its release in the early 60s.

The record has become one of the greatest "one-hit wonders" of all time and it continues to get significant airplay in strong oldies markets like Pittsburgh, Philadelphia, and New York.

Sadly, very little is known about this artist, who passed away too soon at the age of 50. Her name was Bertha Tillman and it's as if she came down from the heavens one day in 1962 and touched us with her soul-stirring, gospel-tinged treasure "**Oh My Angel.**"

 OH MY ANGEL

Open your smartphone camera & scan this QR code to listen to the song.

A GOOD BEAT AND YOU CAN DANCE TO IT

Aired in July 2008

What makes a hit record? There are many theories. The Dick Clark *American Bandstand* theory was that a hit record "had a good beat and you could dance to it." On the business side of things, the ingredients most quoted are timing of release and proper promotion.

Even if you had a song with a good beat that you could dance to and the right promotion with prime time air dates, there was still no guarantee that you had a hit on your hands. In fact, many artists have recorded tunes that they favoured and thought were destined for the top of the charts.

Freddie "Boom Boom" Cannon falls into this category. He cut a record in 1963 that he thought couldn't miss – but it did.

*****

Thanks to his mother, nineteen-year-old Freddie Cannon was able to quit his job as a truck driver in 1959 and start a recording career. What did his mother do for this to happen? She wrote his very first record, "Tallahassee Lassie."

Swan records picked it up, deejay Arnie "Woo Woo" Ginsberg started playing it on his show out of Boston and, in a matter of weeks, the record hit the #6 position on the national pop charts.

Over the next four years, Cannon and the Swan label made it onto the Billboard Hot 100 an additional eighteen times. The most memorable of the tunes were "Way Down Yonder In New Orleans" (#3), "Transistor Sister"(#35), and the Chuck Barris-penned "Palisades Park" (#3).

After he left Swan, Cannon hit it big again on the Warner Brothers label with "Abigail Beecher" in February of 1964 and "Action" in June of 1965. "Action" was the theme song of Dick Clark's TV show *Where The Action Is*, which featured Paul Revere And The Raiders.

One of Cannon's major disappointments in his later years with Swan Records was the poor chart performance of one of his personal favorites that he recorded in the spring of 1963. The record lasted a mere 7 weeks on the charts and failed to get past the 65th position.

Some say, that with the Beatles coming on the scene, the timing of the release was unfortunate. Others say that it sounded too much like his other hits. Still others believe that the song wasn't given enough promotion.

Regardless, Cannon still believes it was one of his best, a song with a great beat about "the girl with the dancing feet," **"Patty Baby."**

 PATTY BABY

Open your smartphone camera & scan this QR code to listen to the song.

MAKING OLD SOUND NEW AND HIP

Aired in January 2010

In the mid-60s, amidst the British Invasion, a quartet from Paterson, New Jersey made a name for themselves thanks to their ability to gain popularity by re-recording hit songs from the past.

One of their nine charted remakes, released in 1967, can be traced back to 1930.

*****

According to lead singer Bob Miranda, the group's original formula was to "take a song that's already proven it could be a hit and put our spin on it."

They first hit the scene in the summer of 1966 with a remake of the Tempos' "See You In September." It went to #3 and remained on the charts for 14 weeks. In the latter part of the same year, they followed up with a cover of Steve Lawrence's "Go Away Little Girl."

They charted again early in 1967 with a version of the classic "Goodnight My Love," a huge R&B hit for Jesse Belvin in 1956. Other covers included "My Mammy" (Al Jolson's theme song written in 1920), "Why Do Fools Fall In Love" (Frankie Lymon & The Teenagers in 1956), "Music! Music! Music!" (Teresa Brewer in 1950), and Neil Sedaka's "Breaking Up Is Hard To Do" from 1962.

Their ability to make the old sound new and hip for the

teenage generation was a testimonial to their name, the Happenings.

In 1967, they took a George and Ira Gershwin tune, written in 1930 for the musical *Girl Crazy* starring Ginger Rogers, and ran it up the charts to the #3 position on the Billboard Hot 100. Prior to this, the song had been recorded by such music legends as Judy Garland, Ethel Merman, and Ella Fitzgerald.

The Happenings' arrangement of the song and the timing of its release proved to be perfect. Perhaps if you asked lead singer, Bob Miranda, why he enjoyed so much success with this record, he might say, "**I Got Rhythm**."

 I GOT RHYTHM

Open your smartphone camera & scan this QR code to listen to the song.

LACKING THE STAYING POWER

Aired in March 2008

One of the most prolific songwriting production teams that came out of the 60s was the team of Jeff Barry and Ellie Greenwich. They honed their skills working in tandem with the likes of Jerry Leiber & Mike Stoller, and the amazing Phil Spector.

Barry and Greenwich have often been considered the trailblazers for the "girl groups" of the early 60s – groups like the Ronettes, the Shangri-Las, the Crystals, and the Dixie Cups come readily to mind.

However, one group that they created instant fame for was an R&B quintet made up of four girls and a guy fresh out of high school. They only cut three records. However, two of them charted with one going Top 10 in the summer of 1964.

*****

Anytime you saw a record on the Redbird label in the 60s, it was a good bet that it was either written or produced by Barry and Greenwich. Teaming together, they worked out of the legendary Brill Building located in the heart of New York City's music district, supplying hit compositions for Phil Spector and Leiber & Stoller.

Barry and Greenwich were attuned to the hearts and minds of Teenage America. In the summer of 1964, they wrote a song for that R&B quintet from Jersey City. This gritty pop record struck a chord with the teen crowd in the summer of 1964 and went to #9 on the Billboard Hot 100.

The group became an overnight success, which led to a grueling tour of one-nighters. As a result, they only managed to cut two more records and never achieved the success that their first release gave them.

Today their hit is one of the forgotten records on the Redbird label even though it ranked right up there with other better-known releases from that era. Some say the group's name, the Jelly Beans, was not a strong one. It certainly was not as strong as their teenage lament, **"I Wanna Love Him So Bad**.*"*

Open your smartphone camera & scan this QR code to listen to the song.

LOOKING COOL IN SCHOOL
Aired in September 2018

Many of us look at September as the beginning of the new year, probably because we spent so many of our impressionable years returning to school in that month.

Going back to school on the first day of each new year was a big deal. For some it was a chance to see school buddies again and get caught up on what they did during the summer.

For others, it was a little nerve racking, especially if you were transitioning to a new school, perhaps going from grade school to high school, or because your family relocated over the summer.

Regardless of what was central to you on your first day, you and your parents made sure you looked your best. Teenagers have remained conscious of their looks, and being cool and in step with fashion continues to be a priority.

In the mid-50s a group from South Carolina sang about an item of clothing that was very "in" during that period.

*****

This "fashion" group was formed in 1955 and had four members — a bass player, a drummer and two singer/guitar players.

Their self-penned "clothing song" was a high energy, Rockabilly-type number that stayed on the Billboard pop charts for over four months, peaking at the 17th position in October of 1957.

The group charted one more time but soon became a one-hit wonder.

However, their one-hit wonder status is understandable, given that at the peak of their careers – 1957 – the age of all four members was from twelve to sixteen. In fact, John Lennon and Ringo Starr were born before these singers, yet these youngsters made it onto the Billboard Hot 100 a decade before the Beatles.

Despite their success, and despite playing on Dick Clark's *American Bandstand* and *The Ed Sullivan Show*, the act was very hard to book because of the members' age – hence finances became a burden for them and the boys headed back to school and, as they put it, "to normal lives."

But they did leave us with a treasure tune, one that included hip teenage expressions like "cool breeze," "crazy little mama" and "cool daddy-o." You will smile as you listen to the forgotten favorite, "**Black Slacks**," by Joe Bennett And The Sparkletones.

 BLACK SLACKS

Open your smartphone camera & scan this QR code to listen to the song.

CARRYING A TORCH FOR SOMEONE

Aired in January 2008

When reminiscing about the early years of Rock & Roll, we often come across songs and artists that were very popular during that time period but for some reason or another have been lost in the shuffle.

In late 1958 a young, good-looking solo artist celebrated his first appearance on the national pop charts in North America. Only nineteen, he would go on to have 25 other recordings make the Billboard Hot 100 in the following seven years with four of them achieving Top 10 status.

*****

After being heard on a *Pet Milk* talent show in Nashville, a young man from Jacksonville, Florida got a chance to audition for Archie Bleyer, the president of Cadence Records. Bleyer signed him and before the close of 1958, our young performer had a double-sided record that made it on the Billboard pop charts.

Two years later, he had his biggest all-time seller – "Poetry In Motion." The artist is Johnny Tillotson, a forgotten favorite of the late 50s and early 60s.

With the exception of "Poetry In Motion," we rarely hear any of Tillotson's records today. That is amazing, given he charted 26 times in a span of seven years from 1958 to 1965. In 1965 he also recorded the popular hit theme song for the TV show *Gidget* starring Sally Field.

Two of his records crossed over to the country charts in 1962 – "It Keeps Right On A-Hurtin'" and his remake of the Hank Lochlin tune "Send Me The Pillow That You Dream On."

Like his two country crossover songs, his second Top 10 recording is sometimes referred to as a torch record, as he sings about his undying love and the burden he would endure "**Without You.**"

 WITHOUT YOU

Open your smartphone camera & scan this QR code to listen to the song.

A CHESS MATCH
Aired in June 2009

In recognition of Father's Day, some attention should be given to an R&B vocal group that was formed at Chicago's Greater Harvest Baptist Church in 1960.

The group went on to record a number of tunes and in addition to being well-known in the Midwest U.S., they were embraced by many in the Carolinas for their beach music style.

The group managed to cross over from the R&B charts to the national pop charts on four occasions while recording for Chess Records.

*****

By 1961 the group had moved away from gospel and began recording R&B. They were turned down by the newly-formed Motown Records and initially by Chess Records.

They eventually signed with Chess and recorded under the tutelage of Billy Davis, Berry Gordy Jr.'s ex-songwriting partner.

Hence, it is probably not surprising that their first release in 1962 sounded a lot like "Shop Around" by Smokey Robinson & The Miracles, which Billy Davis produced while at Motown.

This first release did not do well in many cities across North America. However, it was a hit in Cleveland and did make it onto the Billboard Hot 100 for one week.

That was just the beginning. Chess Records hung in with the group, which went on to record a number of successful R&B tunes and to gather a following on the East Coast with a couple of their records being featured on beach music anthology albums.

When you listen to this first release you will realize that it was not surprising that Billy Davis took this group, the Radiants, under his wing. After all, like the title says, **"Father Knows Best."**

 FATHER KNOWS BEST

Open your smartphone camera & scan this QR code to listen to the song.

THE DIVINE ONE
Aired in June 2001

The goal of record companies is to sell records. When an artist is hot, these companies ride the wave to optimize sales. Sometimes their success can lead to failure when it comes to the releasing of records for airplay.

Choosing the time to release a record is an artform in itself. Companies must balance maximizing the success of one record with releasing another record by the same artist, while maintaining momentum in the marketplace.

In the case of one established artist, the timing of a follow-up record was premature and it ended up lost in shuffle despite its quality and critical acclaim.

***** *

By the late 40s, the reputation of a certain female artist from Newark, New Jersey spread. She began being booked into many of the top clubs throughout the U.S. and Canada. Dubbed "The Divine One," she charted her first record, "It's Magic," in 1948.

Her big break came in 1954 with Mercury Records with her great ballad "Make Yourself Comfortable." It hit the #6 position on the charts as did "Whatever Lola Wants" one year later.

In all, she had 22 singles on the Billboard Hot 100. However, she is best remembered for one record that has become her signature song. It was released in July of 1959 and stayed on the Billboard pop charts for 19 straight weeks, peaking at the #7 position.

The song was so powerful that her next release in November of 1959 didn't receive the attention it should have and only reached the 44th position on the charts. Her sound on this subsequent release is pure and natural.

What else would you expect from the songstress who gave us "Broken-Hearted Melody." The Divine One, Miss Sarah Vaughan, deserved a better fate with her "lost in the shuffle" follow-up recording, "**Smooth Operator.**"

 SMOOTH OPERATOR

Open your smartphone camera & scan this QR code to listen to the song.

RISQUÉ BUT COOL
Aired in March 2014

Back in 1951 there was an R&B group that was making waves regionally but just wasn't ready for prime time because prime time, according to those controlling the airwaves, wasn't ready for them.

This group was in the class of Billy Ward And His Dominoes ("Sixty Minute Man") and, like other R&B performers of the early 50s, had their records labeled as risqué.

*****

Collectors have made this group one of the most beloved of early 50s R&B groups. Their haunting ballads and risqué up-tempo novelty tunes are perennial favorites.

Formed in 1946, this group from Baltimore was originally known as the Oakaleers. They eventually became the Swallows, a name suggested by the mother of one of the group members. It was inspired by her favorite song by the Ink Spots, "When The Swallows Come Back To Capistrano."

This song served as their theme song, but they never got around to recording it, primarily because of the Dominoes' hit version. In the early 50s, legend has it that the Swallows stole the show from singer/actress Pearl Bailey at the Howard Theater in Washington, D.C. with a memorable live performance of the tune.

On December 22, 1951, they received a top rating for

an up-tempo number that unfortunately got categorized as a "race record," meaning it was too racy/risqué to play. Tame by today's standards, the song failed to receive national airplay.

The song also became a Shag dancing favorite in the Carolinas. A long way from Capistrano, the Swallows were flying with "**It Ain't The Meat.**"

 IT AIN'T THE MEAT

Open your smartphone camera & scan this QR code to listen to the song.

JUST FOR
FUN

In the 50s, 60s, and 70s, comedy, in the form of recorded music, found a spot in a marketplace driven by teenagers. Even their parents appreciated these light-hearted recordings that had the ability to put smiles on people's faces.

Single releases on 45s, where humor was the number one purpose, were categorized as novelty records. The ones that appealed to the fans of Rock & Roll would rocket to the top of the charts, only to come crashing down just as fast after reaching their peak.

The following ten moments in time take a jovial and satirical look at a number of things that we were exposed to during the 50s, 60s, and 70s, from junk food, to television, to school, to sports, and the world beyond.

SNACKIN' GOOD
Aired in January 2014

Many New Year's resolutions that we make revolve around losing weight by improving our diet. This moment in time is devoted to one of the great comfort foods that we enjoy year round, the one that many choose to stop eating after the holiday season.

A dedication to this snack food of choice first showed up in a song that was featured on *The Buddy Deane Show* in the early 60s.

*****

Similar to *American Bandstand*, *The Buddy Deane Show* was a dance show for teenagers that aired in Baltimore, Maryland from 1957-1964. Unfortunately, the show was taken off the air: the policy of home station WJZ-TV did not allow the integration of black and white dancers.

A takeoff of the show, dubbed *The Corny Collins Show*, provides the backdrop for the 1988 John Waters movie *Hairspray* starring actor/drag queen Divine (born Harris Glenn Milstead) and future TV host Ricki Lake.

Unfortunately, there is not much footage available from *The Buddy Deane Show*. However, if you look it up on YouTube, you'll find a neat clip from the early 60s of a young girl named Arlene Joy performing a song that she wrote herself. A parody of the classic "Mash Potato" by Dee Dee Sharp, it pays tribute to our snack food of choice.

It is also said to be one of the songs that inspired John Waters to make *Hairspray*.

In December 2007, Joy's self-penned song was featured in *Baltimore Observed: I Want To Believe*, a theatrical performance put on by the graduate students at Baltimore's Towson University who explored the nature and character of the city.

With backup vocals by the original Ink Spots, Arlene Joy's recording is rarely heard today. Perhaps you should not listen to it because it may give you a craving for **"Potato Chips."**

 POTATO CHIPS

Open your smartphone camera & scan this QR code to listen to the song.

THE ELMER FUDD SOUND

Aired in November 2000

One of the most admired TV announcers over the last four decades was Hugh Downs. A key anchor of the popular prime time network show *20/20* in the 90s, Downs made his mark in the early days of TV when he was the original host of the daytime version of the game show *Concentration*, which first aired in the late 50s.

Although never known for his musical prowess, Downs was erroneously credited as being an integral part of a hit record performed by songstress Betty Johnson in 1958.

*****

Johnson, who sang lead on this 1958 hit, had already achieved Top 10 status earlier in her career with "I Dreamed," a song that was released in late 1956.

During the mid to late 50s, Johnson became a regular on the *Jack Parr Show*. As a result, her popularity grew. In 1957, she signed with Atlantic Records and a year later she had what proved to be her biggest hit on that label. Oddly enough, it was a novelty record, but one that lasted four months on the charts. The record is a collector's item, a true lost treasure.

The record? – "The Little Blue Man."

So where does Downs fit into this? Supposedly, he provided the Elmer Fudd-like voice of "The Little Blue Man" whom Betty Johnson dialogues with in the song.

Downs passed away at the age of 99 in 2020. However, his biography makes no mention of his involvement with this recording. According to Johnson's biography, the voice was that of musical theater lyricist Fred Ebb who frequently wrote for performers Liza Minnelli and Chita Rivera. Plus, Ebb co-wrote the song with composer Paul Klein.

A long-time friend and former personal assistant of Ebb's states, "the fact is that Fred Ebb is the voice of the Little Blue Man, not Hugh Downs. They auditioned about 250 different people for the voice" with co-writer Klein proclaiming that no one could do the voice as well as Ebb.

Throughout the song, you can hear Ebb lamenting, "I wuv you! I wuv you!" in his portrayal of "**The Little Blue Man**."

 THE LITTLE
BLUE MAN

Open your smartphone camera & scan this QR code to listen to the song.

BOWING TO THE COMPETITION
Aired in September 2005

In 1961, with interest in street corner harmony beginning to peak, there were a number of singing groups vying for a position on the Billboard pop charts.

One such group, which had established national prominence in 1958, decided to release a novelty tune in 1961 that took a lighter side in recognizing their competition in the music industry.

*****

In late 50s, the Four Preps established themselves as one of the more innovative performing acts in Rock & Roll. Their four-part harmony was exceptional and very apparent in their 1958 release of "Twenty Six Miles Across The Sea" and their follow-up hit "Big Man," which went to #2 and #3 respectively on the Billboard Hot 100.

By 1961 they were competing with a number of similar acts from coast to coast. In a live performance that was subsequently released as a single in 1961, they paid tribute to their counterparts in a comical, yet respectful fashion.

In this "tribute," to the audience's delight, they lampoon the Fleetwoods, the Hollywood Argyles, the Platters, the Four Freshmen, the Kingston Trio, and Dion & The Belmonts.

The live performance, released on Capitol Records, went to #17 on the Billboard Hot 100, #4 on the Billboard

Adult Contemporary chart, and #39 on the UK charts.

In showcasing their talent and capabilities, the Four Preps use their vocal harmonies to honor and parody their contemporaries while seeking "**More Money For You And Me**."

 MORE MONEY FOR YOU AND ME

Open your smartphone camera & scan this QR code to listen to the song.

REALLY, MR. COMO
Aired in October 2000

In the late 50s and early 60s, it was not uncommon for TV and movie personalities to dabble in the music side of things. Some even had hit records. Such was the case with Lorne Greene, better known to many as Ben Cartwright of TV's *Bonanza*, the classic western series of the 60s and early 70s.

Greene, at the peak of his career in 1964, released a ballad that reached the #1 position on the Billboard pop charts. The song was "Ringo," based on a poem he had read, enjoyed, and promptly recorded.

"Ringo" had quite an impact in its time. Two years later, in 1966, a parody of the hit single was performed by another TV personality.

*****

It is estimated that Greene's face was recognizable by more than half a billion people around the world, this statistic based solely on the eighty countries that carried the syndicated *Bonanza*.

Prior to acting, Greene, a Canadian, was a radio announcer with the Canadian Broadcasting Corporation (CBC). For three years during World War II, his commanding voice meant nothing but bad news for Canadian listeners and earned him the title "The Voice Of Doom."

It was this same powerful baritone voice that helped propel "Ringo" to #1 on December 5, 1964.

In 1966, a TV personality by the name of Frank Gallop came out with his parody of "Ringo." Gallop was probably best known as the announcer for Perry Como's TV show. He, too, had a very deep voice, heard in his trademark, "Really, Mr. Como."

In fact, the word "Really" can be heard at the conclusion of the parody of Lorne Greene's hit record. The parody, which made it to #34 on the Billboard Hot 100, is titled **"The Ballad Of Irving."**

THE BALLAD OF IRVING

Open your smartphone camera & scan this QR code to listen to the song.

A SATIRICAL TRIBUTE
Aired in January 2002

Social comment records, also known as "protest songs," were common in the mid-60s. Included in this genre were songs like "Eve Of Destruction" in 1965 by Barry McGuire, "Society's Child" by Janis Ian in 1967, and "For What It's Worth" by Buffalo Springfield, also in 1967.

However, social comment records were not without their satirical side.

*****

McGuire's "Eve Of Destruction" stayed on the Billboard Hot 100 for 11 weeks, peaking at the #1 position the week of September 25, 1965. Backed by the original members of the Grass Roots on the recording, McGuire was one of first artists signed to the newly formed Dunhill label.

From 1962 through early 1965, McGuire had sung lead for The New Christy Minstrels on their hits "Green, Green" and "Saturday Night." He also penned "Greenback Dollar" for the Kingston Trio.

While McGuire's career was on the rise, so was that of an English wonder boy by the name of Jonathan King. In 1965 he, too, had a smash hit. Entitled "Everyone's Gone To The Moon," the song also charted in North America, hitting the Billboard pop charts the same week that "Eve Of Destruction" made it to #1.

This was just the beginning for King, as he went on to become not only a singer but also a songwriter, producer, TV personality, talent agent, disc jockey, and record company owner. Among his subsequent discoveries were Genesis, the Bay City Rollers, and 10cc.

In 1966, King had some fun by putting five British Royal Air Force recruits together to sing a tongue-in-cheek protest song that he had written, lampooning the media's obsession with reporting bad news. He called the group Hedgehoppers Anonymous, and they took great "pleasure" singing about bombings and controversial medical advancements in their 1966 satirical tribute to the times, **"It's Good News Week."**

Open your smartphone camera & scan this QR code to listen to the song.

CAMPUS CLOWNS
Aired in April 2015

This moment in time deals with a novelty record that was a one-hit wonder. It came out in 1960, reaching the 8th position on the Billboard Hot 100. One interesting thing about this tune is that it was inspired by a character from a TV cartoon show.

*****

At Adelphi College in Garden City, Long Island, three students formed a singing group in late 1959. Given the school was ivy-covered, they decided to call themselves the Ivy Three. The group consisted of Charlie Cane, Artie Berk, and Don Rubin.

The group did not stay together long with Berk becoming an insurance salesman while Rubin and Cane (under his birth name Koppelman) would go on to become a successful production team in the music industry, working with the likes of Petula Clark, the Turtles, Lovin' Spoonful, and Gary Lewis.

The Ivy Three's success had a lot to do with timing. Encouraged by friends, the trio made their way to Shell Recordings in Manhattan, New York, where they met the songwriting team of Lou Stallman and Sid Jacobson. The songwriters were in the midst of writing a novelty tune based on Yogi Bear, a TV cartoon character featured on *The Huckleberry Hound Show*. By January of 1961, Yogi

Bear had his own TV show and remained in the public eye, stealing picnic baskets until 1988.

Stallman and Jacobson's willingness to spend some time with the trio and incorporate Cane's song suggestions resulted in a 1960 collaboration that went Top 10.

After releasing "Hush Little Baby," a non-novelty follow-up tune, two additional comedy-like singles, "Nine Out of Ten" and "Bagoo," went nowhere. The Ivy Three disbanded.

However, the trio did manage to get their fifteen minutes of fame as recording artists thanks to a cartoon character by the name of "**Yogi**."

Open your smartphone camera & scan this QR code to listen to the song.

THE NAME GAME
Aired in April 2013

Throughout the 50s, 60s, and 70s, songs with names in them proved to be quite successful. We had Dion singing about "Runaround Sue" (#1 - 1961), Shelley Fabares dreaming about "Johnny Angel" (#1 - 1962), Marcie Blane wanting to be "Bobby's Girl" (#3 - 1962), and the Marvelettes warning us "Don't Mess With Bill" (#7 - 1966), to "name" a few.

In 1964, R&B singer/songwriter Shirley Ellis got into the act, penning a song that went to #3 on the charts the following year. In the recording, through speaking and singing, Ellis explains how to play a rhyming game using people's names. Titled "The Name Game," this record has been covered by dozens of artists and has become a popular children's singalong.

Charting prior to the above examples, there was a fun song or "novelty record" that cleverly used names out of context. It was released in 1960 by a well-established artist who also had his own TV show at the time.

*****

The record itself was a little different from other records that had people's names associated with them because the names mentioned in this record identified various states in the U.S. These state names were used creatively in the form of extended puns. This "pun" song went to #22 on Billboard Hot 100 and remained on the charts for 11 weeks.

Who would have thought that a former barber turned singer from Pennsylvania with twelve prior Top 10 hits, three of which went to #1, would venture out of his comfort zone and do a novelty tune. But that's what Perry Como did when he recorded "**Delaware.**"

Epilogue: Fifteen states are mentioned in the song – Delaware, New Jersey, California, Hawaii, Mississippi, Minnesota, Oregon, Alaska, Texas, Wisconsin, Nebraska, Arkansas, Tennessee, Florida, and Missouri.

 DELAWARE

Open your smartphone camera & scan this QR code to listen to the song.

IT CAME FROM THE SKY

Aired in June 2018

During Rock & Roll's first decade, the late 50s and early 60s, westerns ruled "television land" in North America, so much so, that nearly all prime time TV was dedicated to them.

One of the more successful and remembered shows was *Rawhide*, which starred Eric Fleming as trail boss Gil Favor. It also featured an upcoming actor who played trailhand Rowdy Yates. This actor would go on to become a megastar and a top director. His name ... Clint Eastwood.

Rawhide first aired on January 9, 1959 and enjoyed a seven-year run. While Fleming and Eastwood were front and center in most episodes, there was a supporting actor in the cast who had garnered national recognition as a singer/songwriter in 1958, while rehearsing his role as scout Pete Nolan in *Rawhide*. In fact, this supporting actor had a #1 record in June of 1958.

*****

Joining the *Rawhide* cast gave the singer/songwriter little time to promote his song. As it turned out, he didn't have to. The success of his song led to a huge amount of merchandising including hats with horns, tee shirts, and even ice cream.

Subsequent to his *Rawhide* days, he began writing and recording parodies using the name Ben Colder, his alter ego. Five of his parodies charted, including "Don't Go Near The Eskimos," a 1962 parody of Rex Allen's hit record, "Don't Go Near The Indians."

He also wrote the theme song for the TV show *Hee Haw*, and in the late 60s and early 70s he became a regular on the show, playing a drunken country songwriter.

Despite his accomplished career, this talented singer, songwriter, and actor is still best remembered for that #1 song in June of 1958.

Imagine what parents had to put up with if they gave birth at the time this Sheb Wooley song was a big hit. Picture older siblings joking with their friends by announcing that their mother had given birth to "a one-eyed, one-horned, flyin' **Purple People Eater**."

 PURPLE PEOPLE EATER

Open your smartphone camera & scan this QR code to listen to the song.

MOUSE TRAP

Aired in November 2009

On October 23, 2009, one of the great, zany comedians of all time died at the age of 83. His television show was a hit with kids and teens in the 50s and 60s, with his offbeat humor and antics often getting him and his crew into trouble.

His talents were not confined to television, however. He recorded a number of chart-topping albums and gave live performances on Broadway, in dinner theaters, and at comedy clubs. In the late 1960s, he became a regular on one of TV's most popular programs, *What's My Line?*, where he stayed for seven years.

Throughout the 1970s, he lent his wacky sense of humor to numerous game and variety shows, including *Jr. Almost Anything Goes*, *Sha Na Na*, and *Bloopers And Practical Jokes*.

His ability to get onto the Billboard pop charts with a single in 1965 is remarkable given that it was during the British Invasion, and the song was basically a "dance record," a genre that had been beaten to death throughout the early 60s.

*****

Born Milton Supman on January 8, 1926 in Franklinton, North Carolina, the youngest of three sons, this soon-to-become slapstick specialist grew up in Huntington, West Virginia and received his B.A. in journalism from Marshall University. He landed a local job as a radio scriptwriter after college, moonlighting as a comedian. The radio station eventually moved him on air and he became the top-rated deejay in the area.

After moving to Detroit in 1953, he quickly became a popular television personality, especially among young audiences.

After seven years in Detroit, he moved to the West Coast where his TV show became Los Angeles' #1 show, attracting such guest stars as Frank Sinatra and Sammy Davis Jr. He was beloved by viewers as much for his wild personality as his signature pie-throwing antics.

He moved his show to New York City in 1964; it was syndicated throughout the United States, Canada, Australia, and New Zealand during the next two years.

One of his most notorious stunts occurred in 1964, when he jokingly told his young audience to "take some of those green pieces of paper with pictures of George Washington, Benjamin Franklin, Lincoln, and Jefferson on them" from their parents' wallets and send them to him. Several viewers did send him some money, but all funds were returned. Though he was suspended from television for a week, the stunt actually boosted his ratings.

Many know Milton Supman better by his stage name, Soupy Sales. In the mid-60s whatever "Soupy Sez" was golden. In 1965, his followers got him onto the Billboard Hot 100 by obeying him and buying his record while being lured to dance "**The Mouse**."

 THE MOUSE

Open your smartphone camera & scan this QR code to listen to the song.

FOR THE LOVE OF THE GAME
Aired in June 2005

The date: August 12, 1956. Comedian Phil Silvers hosts *The Ed Sullivan Show*, filling in for an ailing Ed Sullivan who is recuperating from a car accident. Much of the show is a tribute to the New York Yankees and their wives, many of whom appear live on the show.

During the telecast, one of the more prominent players on the Yankees is featured doing a duet with pop singer Teresa Brewer.

*****

In 2002, *The Ed Sullivan Show* was ranked #15 in *TV Guide's 50 Greatest TV Shows of All Time*. Originally called *The Toast of the Town*, it became a must-see show on CBS, spanning four decades from 1948 – 1971 and holding down the 8:00 – 9:00 pm time slot on Sunday nights.

A true variety show, it featured all types of entertainment from comedians to circus acts to popular recording artists. If you made it on the show, you were a somebody and it would enhance your career – just ask the Beatles who made their North American debut on this show on February 9, 1964, in front of an estimated 73 million viewers.

Prior to hosting his own show, Sullivan was a sportswriter in New York City. Throughout his TV career, he often honored or recognized sports celebrities who were sitting in the audience. How ironic that he was not able to host that August 1956 show.

At the time, Teresa Brewer was at the peak of her career with four Top 10 songs including two #1 hits ("Music! Music! Music!" [1950] and "Till I Waltz With You Again" [1952]). Her duet that evening was a tribute tune that she had co-written that summer after attending a Yankee baseball game. She even convinced a Yankee ballplayer to participate in the recording of it. Today this single is one of the most collectible of all Brewer's records.

That Yankee who was part of the onstage duet was Mickey Mantle, who probably would have preferred to be standing at the plate readying himself to hit a fastball rather than being part of this performance. But he endured, as Teresa Brewer paid tribute to him with her light-hearted novelty tune, **"I Love Mickey."**

Epilogue: For you sports buffs, Mickey Mantle went on to have one of his best years in 1956, winning MVP honors and the Triple Crown of baseball by leading the league in batting average (.353), homeruns (52), and runs batted in (130). The Yankees would go on to win yet another World Series that year.

 I LOVE MICKEY

Open your smartphone camera & scan this QR code to listen to the song.

My good friend from the film industry, Herb Dow, has had a passion for peanut butter since he was a little boy. Meeting Sorrells Pickard (yes, his real name) who grew

up on a peanut farm in Lovedale, Florida, was kismet for Herb. Together, they were responsible for creating a peanut butter that stood out from all the rest.

Sorrells' unique style of country music, combined with his warm Southern charm, made him the perfect spokesperson for their Sorrells Pickard Gourmet Peanut Butter brand (SPGPB).

In marketing this product, both Sorrells and Herb knew that, to be successful, they would have to touch the hearts of all lovers of peanut butter. With their approval, I began exploring unconventional marketing opportunities that would assist in "spreading" the word and differentiating the brand. Internet radio proved to be one such opportunity. In August 2000, SPGPB became the proud sponsor of *Treasure Island Oldies*.

Peanut butter lover Michael Godin, the host of the show, and I decided to create a weekly feature to showcase this sponsorship. What resulted was the tongue-twisting "Sorrells Pickard Gourmet Peanut Butter Pick Of The

Week," a five-minute walk down memory lane that included a song from the past, an anecdote surrounding the song, and of course, the SPGPB jingle.

Sorrells' untimely passing on July 5, 2003 was a shock to all of us involved with the evolution of his and Herb's dream brand. As a result, SPGPB soon folded.

Despite not being a household name, Sorrells, who was also a performer and songwriter, would be the first to tell you how much he enjoyed his life in the entertainment industry and how fortunate he was to rub elbows with some of the greats. In his words, "When you live your dream, you have accomplished a lot."

As an actor, he co-starred in such films as *Hardbodies* and *Hardbodies 2*, and had major roles in *Ultraviolet* with Esai Morales, *Lucky Thirteen* with Eric Stolz, and *W.W. and the Dixie Dancekings* with Burt Reynolds.

As a singer/songwriter, he had more than 100 of his songs recorded by country artists including Roy Clark, Slim Whitman, Hank Thompson, Kitty Wells, and The Statler Brothers. Ringo Starr included four of Sorrells' original songs on his classic *Beaucoups of Blues* album, recorded in Nashville in the early 70s.

Beginning with live radio shows and then onto the stage of the Grand Ole Opry, he toured extensively, playing virtually every major city in the United States and Canada. In Canada, he toured and played with the legendary Buddy Knox, of "Party Doll" fame.

However, one of his fondest memories dates back to Nashville in the late 70s when he, along with session musician Bucky Barrett, got together with their pals Waylon Jennings, Kris Kristofferson, and Billy Swan. Sorrells once described this onstage performance as only Sorrells could – in his deep Southern drawl, the bass singer simply said, "It was mighty good." I will always remember Sorrells when I hear "**Goodnight Irene**."

 GOODNIGHT IRENE

Open your smartphone camera & scan this QR code to listen to the song.

ACKNOWLEDGEMENTS

"It takes a village to raise a child"
– Old African Proverb

One person can write a book, but it takes many committed people to breathe life into it and get its message out. In this regard, I owe a tremendous amount of thanks to my production team, my family, and my friends and supporters.

Leading the way has been the team at The Self Publishing Agency headed up by Megan Williams. Thanks to the agency, I was introduced to Trevor McMonagle who became my editor, a man whose skills mirror his mantra of "the right words, in the right place, at the right time." In tandem with this, a big *salute* to my wife, Cindy Williams, who reviewed and commented on everything Trevor and I produced.

When it comes to book design and layout, I was fortunate to partner up with Kristy Twellmann Hill whose creativity and can-do attitude made this part of the journey most enjoyable.

I thank Michael Godin for his trust in me over these years to deliver stories that would resonate with his listening audience. A special shout-out to them and the faithful in the *Treasure Island Oldies* chatroom, affectionately known as the "nuts in the hut."

I have been blessed with the support and encouragement from my colleagues in the entertainment industry and, in particular, my International Quorum of Motion Picture Producers family.

I also feel very honoured for the support and contributions from Norm N. Nite, Mike Benz, David Spero, Curt Hahn, Dan Koch, and Sorrells Pickard Gourmet Peanut Butter co-founder Herb Dow.

My thanks to Brothers Martin Silver, Bill Anderson, Doug Hann, Craig Freifeld, Peter Badali, Jeff Ross, and the rest of the Gamma Sigma Fraternity International alumni for their encouragement.

And a "high five" to my brother, Allan, for sharing his expertise in marketing, promotion, and distribution. And to my daughter, Cathy, the keeper of my manuscripts.

Lastly, a tip of the needle to my friends and colleagues who have always been there for me – Paul Airey, Jane Baer, David Boxer, Ted Cowie, Rob Evans, Peter Fentiman, Judy Harnett, Kalvin Houde, Rodney Jacobs, Roger Jones, Don Laird, Darrell Lidstone, Phil Mackesy, Colleen McGuinness, Peter Meredith, Carol Milne, Brian Murphy, Red Robinson, Kileen Tucker Scott, Jim & Maureen Tusty, Glenn Williams, Jim Winters, Dale Wolfe, Darryl Wolf, Gary Wong, et al.

SOURCES

Brewster, Bill and Broughton, Frank. *Last Night A DJ Saved My Life.* New York: Grove Press, 2006.

Bronson, Fred. *The Billboard Book Of Number One Hits.* New York: Billboard Publications, Inc., 1988.

Clark, Dick and Robinson, Richard. *Rock, Roll & Remember.* New York: Thomas Y. Crowell Company, 1976.

Cohn, Nik. *A WopBopaLooBopLopBamBoom.* Boulder, Colorado: Paladin Pres 1972.

Hall, Ron. *The CHUM Chart Book 1957 – 1986.* Toronto: Stardust Productions Inc., 2007.

Jancik, Wayne. *The Billboard Book Of One-Hit Wonders Revised and Expanded.* New York: Watson-Guptill Publications, 1998.

Miller, Jim. *The Rolling Stone Illustrated History Of Rock & Roll.* New York: Random House, 1976.

Nite, Norm N. *Rock On: The Illustrated Encyclopedia Of Rock N' Roll – The Solid Gold Years.* New York: Thomas Y. Crowell Company, 1974.

Nite, Norm N. *Rock On: Volume II, The Illustrated Encyclopedia Of Rock N' Roll – The Modern Years: 1964 - Present.* New York: Thomas Y. Crowell Company, 1978.

Nite, Norm N. *The House That Rock Built*. Kent, Ohio: The Kent State University Press, 2020.

Robinson, Red and Hodgins, Peggy. Rockbound: *Rock 'N' Roll Encounters 1955 to 1969*. Surrey, BC: Hancock House Publishers Ltd., 1983.

Shore, Michael and Clark, Dick. *The History of American Bandstand*. New York: Ballantine Books, 1985.

Smith, Wes. *The Pied Pipers of Rock 'N' Roll: Radio Deejays of the 50s and 60s*. Atlanta: Longstreet Press, Inc., 1989.

Warner, Jay. *American Singing Groups – A History From 1940 To Today*. Milwaukee. Hal Leonard Corporation, 2006.

Whitburn, Joel. *Top Country Singles 1944 – 1988*. Menomonee Falls, Wisconsin. Record Research Inc., 1989.

Whitburn, Joel. *Top Pop Singles 1940 – 1955*. Menomonee Falls, Wisconsin. Record Research Inc., 1973.

Whitburn, Joel. *Top Pop Singles 1955 – 1999*. Menomonee Falls, Wisconsin. Record Research Inc., 2000.

Wikipedia. Various articles on recordings and performers in the music industry.

ABOUT THE AUTHOR

Tom Locke lives in Vancouver, B.C., Canada, spending the majority of his time writing and executive producing in the entertainment industry. Over the past 25 years, Tom has also studied and consulted on the impact of digital technology in business. It was during this period of time that he introduced the online world to his music creation, "Moments In Time."

He has a passion for music. Writing this book was a natural for him as he was weaned on the music of the 50s, 60s, and 70s while growing up in Toronto. The book became a reality thanks to the online listening audience at *Treasure Island Oldies,* who encouraged Tom to share his impeccably researched music segments that he has produced on a weekly basis for this show since August 2000.

You can reach Tom by email at <u>tomlocke@MITstories.com</u>

**More "Moments In Time" to come
... STAY TUNED**

Printed in Great Britain
by Amazon